ELIMINATE NEGATIVE THINKING

THE 10-STEP BLUEPRINT TO OVERCOME SELF-DOUBT, REWIRE YOUR BRAIN AND BUILD EMOTIONAL RESILIENCE, CRUSH NEGATIVITY AND ACHIEVE INNER PEACE

JULIA DELOACH

© **Copyright 2025 - All rights reserved.**

The content contained within this book may not be reproduced, duplicated or transmitted without direct written permission from the author or the publisher.

Under no circumstances will any blame or legal responsibility be held against the publisher, or author, for any damages, reparation, or monetary loss due to the information contained within this book, either directly or indirectly.

Legal Notice:

This book is copyright protected. It is only for personal use. You cannot amend, distribute, sell, use, quote or paraphrase any part, or the content within this book, without the consent of the author or publisher.

Disclaimer Notice:

Please note the information contained within this document is for educational and entertainment purposes only. All effort has been executed to present accurate, up to date, reliable, complete information. No warranties of any kind are declared or implied. Readers acknowledge that the author is not engaged in the rendering of legal, financial, medical or professional advice. The content within this book has been derived from various sources. Please consult a licensed professional before attempting any techniques outlined in this book.

By reading this document, the reader agrees that under no circumstances is the author responsible for any losses, direct or indirect, that are incurred as a result of the use of the information contained within this document, including, but not limited to, errors, omissions, or inaccuracies.

Meridian Hills Publishing

Hardcover ISBN: 979-8-89754-017-4

Paperback ISBN: 979-8-89754-018-1

E-Book ISBN: 979-8-89754-019-8

CONTENTS

Introduction	5
1. IDENTIFYING COGNITIVE DISTORTIONS	9
Common Cognitive Distortions	10
2. CHALLENGING NEGATIVE THOUGHTS	18
Introduce Techniques to Question and Challenge Negative Thoughts	19
The Importance of Evidence-Based Thinking	24
3. DEVELOPING A GRATITUDE PRACTICE	32
How Gratitude Shifts Focus From Negativity to Appreciation	33
The Science-Backed Benefits of Gratitude	35
Different Gratitude Practices	37
4. PRACTICING MINDFULNESS AND MEDITATION	46
How Mindfulness Helps Manage Negative Thoughts	47
Basic Meditation Techniques for Awareness	49
Breathwork: A Fast-Acting Tool for Breaking Negative Thought Loops	53
5. ENGAGING IN POSITIVE ACTIVITIES	60
Importance of Participating in Activities	61
How Hobbies and Interests Can Counteract Negative Thinking	63
6. BUILDING SELF-COMPASSION	72
What Is Self-Compassion?	72
Practices to Cultivate Kindness Toward Oneself	75
7. UTILIZING RELAXATION TECHNIQUES	87
How Relaxation Techniques Reduce Stress and Negative Thinking	88
Effective Relaxation Techniques	89
Havening: Rewiring Your Emotional Responses	91
8. SEEKING SOCIAL SUPPORT	102
Importance of Connecting With Others	103
Exercises to Build Social Connections	107

9. SETTING REALISTIC GOALS 114
   The Role of Goal-Setting in Fostering a Positive
   Mindset 115
   SMART Goals 117

10. MAINTAINING PROGRESS AND PREVENTING
    RELAPSE 127
    Importance of Ongoing Practice and Self-Awareness 128
    Strategies to Sustain Positive Changes and Handle
    Setbacks 131

Conclusion 141
Bibliography 145

INTRODUCTION

Negative thinking is like an invisible force that shapes your reality, influencing how you see yourself, how you interpret the world, and even how you interact with others. It's subtle, often disguised as self-protection, yet powerful enough to dictate your decisions, limit your potential, and keep you trapped in a cycle of self-doubt and anxiety. If you've ever hesitated to take a leap because you were convinced you'd fail, replayed past mistakes in your head until they felt unbearable, or assumed the worst before anything even happened, you've experienced the weight of negative thinking.

At its core, negative thinking is a cognitive habit, a pattern of interpreting experiences in a way that fuels fear, uncertainty, and limitation. It manifests in many forms: self-doubt that convinces you you're not good enough, catastrophizing that makes every setback feel like a disaster, and overgeneralization that leads you to believe one failure defines your entire future. It makes you believe in worst-case scenarios, magnifies insecurities, and drowns out possibilities with a relentless stream of criticism (Ridsdel, 2023). Over time, it doesn't just shape your thoughts; it rewires your brain to expect failure, disappointment, and rejection, turning these into self-fulfilling prophecies.

The consequences of persistent negative thinking extend far beyond mood swings or fleeting moments of self-doubt. On a mental level, it breeds anxiety, stress, and depression, disrupting your ability to focus, make decisions, and engage in meaningful relationships. You become hyper-aware of potential threats, real or imagined, and your mind gets stuck in a loop of overanalyzing, second-guessing, and anticipating the worst. Instead of seeing challenges as opportunities for growth, you view them as evidence of your inadequacy (Ridsdel, 2023). Rather than embracing uncertainty with curiosity, you fear it as a path to inevitable failure.

But here's the truth: negative thinking is not a fixed part of your identity. It's not an unchangeable trait or an inevitable burden you must carry for life. The mind is not static; it's adaptable, capable of growth, and, most importantly, changing itself. This is where the science of neuroplasticity changes everything.

Neuroplasticity refers to the brain's ability to reorganize itself by forming new neural connections in response to experiences, thoughts, and behaviors. For years, scientists believed the brain's structure was largely fixed after childhood, but research now shows that your thoughts have the power to physically reshape your brain. The more you engage in a particular thought pattern (whether positive or negative), the stronger the neural pathways associated with that thought become. Imagine carving a path through a dense forest (Marzola et al., 2023). The more you walk the same route, the clearer and more defined the path becomes. This is exactly how thoughts work in your brain. Repeated negative thinking strengthens neural circuits that support doubt, fear, and self-criticism. However, just as a new path can be created through a forest, new thought patterns can be created in your brain, and old, harmful patterns can be weakened.

This means that no matter how deeply adopted negative thinking feels, it is possible to break free. You are not at the mercy of your thoughts; you have the power to change your mindset and develop a healthier, more constructive way of thinking. It won't happen overnight, but with the right tools and consistent effort, you can shift your mental landscape and free yourself from the grip of self-defeating beliefs.

This book, *Eliminate Negative Thinking*, is your guide to that change. The 10-step blueprint outlined in these pages is designed to help you systematically identify, challenge, and replace negative thought patterns with empowering, growth-oriented thinking. You'll learn how to recognize the hidden triggers fueling your self-doubt, how to break the cycle of overthinking and fear, and how to develop resilience in the face of setbacks. More importantly, you'll discover how to grow inner peace, not by eliminating challenges from your life but by changing the way you respond to them.

The first step is understanding that negative thinking is not who you are. It's simply a habit. Like any habit, it can be changed. Let's begin!

1

IDENTIFYING COGNITIVE DISTORTIONS

Have you ever caught yourself thinking, *I always mess things up* or, *No one ever listens to me*? These kinds of thoughts feel real in the moment, but are they actually true? If you take a step back, you might realize they're exaggerated, unfair, or even completely false. These are called cognitive distortions, deeply ingrained patterns of thinking that warp reality, fuel negativity, and keep you stuck in cycles of self-doubt and frustration.

You might not even realize how often these distortions sneak into your thoughts. Maybe you assume the worst before giving a situation a fair chance. Perhaps you filter out every positive thing someone says and focus only on the one minor criticism. Or you blame yourself for something that wasn't entirely in your control. These distortions shape how you see yourself, others, and the world around you, and over time, they can chip away at your confidence and peace of mind.

The tricky part is that your brain believes these thoughts are helpful. It's trying to protect you: preparing you for disappointment, shielding you from embarrassment, or making sense of a complicated world. But instead of helping, these patterns often trap you in unnecessary fear, anger, or sadness. The good news is that once you recognize these distortions for what they are (mental habits, not absolute truths), you can start challenging them.

Identifying cognitive distortions is the first step in breaking free from negative thinking. When you begin to notice them, you create space for healthier, more balanced thoughts to take their place. So, are you ready to uncover the hidden patterns in your mind and take back control of your perspective?

Let's begin.

COMMON COGNITIVE DISTORTIONS

Now that you know how cognitive distortions can shape your thoughts and emotions, it's time to look at the mental filters that come in many forms, each with its own way of twisting reality. Some lead you to see the world in black and white, while others convince you that one bad moment defines your entire life. The more you understand these distortions, the better you can spot them in real time and challenge them before they take control (Stanborough, 2022).

All-or-Nothing Thinking

- Do you find yourself dismissing small achievements because they don't meet an impossibly high standard?
- Have you ever felt like one mistake defines your entire ability or worth in a certain area?
- Do you struggle to recognize progress unless it's a complete success?
- When faced with setbacks, do you feel tempted to give up entirely rather than adjust and keep going?
- Have you ever felt like anything less than perfect is a failure?

That's all-or-nothing thinking, also known as black-and-white thinking. It pushes you into extremes—success or failure, good or bad, worthy or unworthy—without any middle ground. If you don't ace that work presentation, you will convince yourself it was a disaster (Stanborough, 2022). If you slip up on your diet, you decide the entire effort is pointless.

This kind of thinking creates an unrealistic standard that no one can meet. Life is full of shades of gray, and expecting perfection only sets you up for disappointment. Instead of acknowledging progress or partial successes, all-or-nothing thinking makes you feel like nothing is ever enough.

Overgeneralization

One mistake, one rejection, one tough day, and suddenly, you believe this always happens to you or that things will never get better. Overgeneralization takes a single event and applies it to your entire life, as if one bad experience is proof that the future will be just as bleak (Stanborough, 2022).

Imagine you bomb a job interview. Instead of recognizing it as just one setback, you think, *I'm terrible at interviews. I'll never get hired anywhere.* Or maybe a friend cancels plans, and your mind jumps to, *People always let me down. I can't trust anyone.* Over time, this distortion convinces you that your struggles are permanent when, in reality, they're just temporary bumps in the road.

Catastrophizing

Your boss wants to talk to you, and immediately, your mind races:

- *What if I'm in trouble?*
- *What if I get fired?*
- *What if I get insulted in front of everyone?*
- *What if everyone starts mocking me?*
- *What if I can't find another job?*

This is catastrophizing—assuming the worst-case scenario without real evidence (Stanborough, 2022). It's like your brain is on a runaway train, speeding toward disaster when the destination is still unknown.

This distortion turns minor problems into major crises. A small disagreement in a relationship suddenly feels like a breakup. A headache must mean a serious illness. The tiniest mistake becomes a sign that everything is falling apart. When you catastrophize, you spend energy worrying about things that haven't even happened, often at the expense of handling what's actually in front of you.

Mental Filtering

- Have you ever had a great day but fixated on one small thing that went wrong?
- Do you replay negative moments in your mind even when the rest of the day was positive?
- When someone gives you a compliment, do you tend to focus more on their criticism instead?
- Do you feel like one mistake or setback overshadows all your successes?
- Have you ever downplayed your achievements because you were too focused on what still needed improvement?

That's mental filtering in progress. You ignore the positive and zoom in on the negative. Even when you receive praise, your brain locks onto the one piece of criticism (Stanborough, 2022). Even if most of your life is going well, you obsess over the one problem you haven't solved yet.

This distortion creates a biased perception of reality. You might achieve something important but still feel like a failure because you focus only on what didn't go right. Over time, mental filtering drains your motivation and self-worth because it convinces you that nothing is ever good enough.

Discounting the Positive

Similar to mental filtering, discounting the positive takes good experiences and downplays them (Stanborough, 2022). Someone compliments you, and you brush it off: "They're just being nice." You accomplish a goal, but you tell yourself it wasn't a big deal. Even when others acknowledge your strengths, you assume they're exaggerating.

This distortion keeps you from fully appreciating your achievements and strengths. Instead of letting positive experiences build confidence, you dismiss them as flukes or luck. But just because your brain tries to minimize success doesn't mean it isn't real.

Personalization and Blame

Personalization is when you take responsibility for things that aren't actually your fault (Stanborough, 2022). Your partner seems quiet during dinner, and you immediately think, *They must be mad at me*, rather than considering they might just be tired or preoccupied. Your child has a bad day at school, and you blame yourself, thinking, *I should have done more as a parent*, rather than acknowledging that kids have tough days too.

This distortion makes you feel guilty for things beyond your control, leading to unnecessary stress and self-blame.

On the flip side, there's also the tendency to blame others entirely for negative outcomes. Instead of acknowledging a mix of circumstances, you might think, *It's all their fault!* Whether you personalize or blame, both distortions prevent you from seeing situations clearly and fairly.

Emotional Reasoning

If you feel worthless, you assume you are worthless. If you feel like something bad is going to happen, you believe it will happen. Emotional reasoning takes feelings and treats them as facts, even when they aren't based on reality (Stanborough, 2022).

This is dangerous because feelings can be misleading. Feeling anxious doesn't necessarily mean you're in danger. Feeling unlovable doesn't mean no one cares about you. Just because your emotions are strong doesn't mean they're an accurate reflection of the truth.

Labeling and Mislabeling

Instead of seeing mistakes as part of being human, labeling slaps a permanent, negative identity onto yourself or others (Stanborough, 2022). If you fail a test, you think, *I'm stupid.* If someone makes a rude comment, you decide *they're a terrible person.* Instead of evaluating actions, this distortion assigns a fixed, negative label that leaves no room for change.

Mislabeling takes it a step further, using exaggerated or emotionally loaded language (Stanborough, 2022). Instead of saying, "I made a mistake, you tell yourself, I'm a complete failure." Instead of thinking, *That person was rude today,* you say, *They're the worst human beings ever.* This type of thinking fuels resentment, self-hatred, and unrealistic expectations of both yourself and others.

Should Statements

Do you ever catch yourself saying, *I should be more successful by now,* or *People should always be kind*?

Should statements create rigid, unrealistic rules about yourself, others, and the world (Stanborough, 2022). When life doesn't align with these expectations, frustration, guilt, and disappointment follow.

Telling yourself "I should never feel anxious or I should always be happy" ignores the complexity of emotions. Expecting "People should never let me down" overlooks human imperfections. While setting standards is important, should statements often create unnecessary stress by demanding perfection where it isn't possible.

Jumping to Conclusions

This distortion has two main forms: mind reading and fortune telling (Stanborough, 2022).

- Mind reading happens when you assume you know what others are thinking without evidence. If a coworker doesn't respond quickly, you assume, *They think I'm incompetent.*

- Fortune-telling is predicting negative outcomes without proof. You convince yourself, *I'll never get this promotion,* or *This date is going to be a disaster,* even though you have no real reason to believe it.

Both forms of jumping to conclusions create unnecessary worry and strain relationships by making you react to assumptions instead of reality.

Thought Diary—Track Your Daily Thoughts

One of the most effective ways to identify cognitive distortions is by keeping a thought diary. When you track your daily thoughts, you start to recognize patterns in how you interpret situations, emotions, and challenges. This awareness is the first step in changing negative thinking habits and replacing them with more balanced perspectives.

A thought diary helps you slow down and analyze your thoughts rather than accepting them as absolute truth. It allows you to see how your mind processes experiences and where distortions may be influencing your emotions and reactions. By writing down your thoughts consistently, you gain insight into recurring negative patterns, making it easier to challenge and reframe them.

Instructions

1. **Choose a notebook or digital tool:** Use a notebook, journal, or a notes app on your phone—whatever feels most comfortable for you. The key is to have a space where you can quickly write down your thoughts each day.
2. **Set aside time daily:** Spend at least five to ten minutes each day recording your thoughts. It's best to do this at a consistent time, such as in the evening when reflecting on the day or right after experiencing a strong emotional reaction.
3. **Record the situation:** Start by describing what happened. Be as objective as possible. Write down the facts of the situation without adding your emotions or interpretations just yet. For

example: "I sent a message to a friend, and they didn't respond all day."
4. **Write down your initial thought:** Note the first thought that came to your mind in response to the situation. Be honest, even if the thought feels irrational or exaggerated. For instance, "They're ignoring me because they don't like me anymore."
5. **Identify the cognitive distortion:** Look at the list of common cognitive distortions and see if your thought fits into one of them. Are you jumping to conclusions, catastrophizing, or engaging in all-or-nothing thinking? You can identify that "This is mind reading because I'm assuming I know what they're thinking without any proof."
6. **Describe how the thought made you feel**: Write down the emotions that came up when you had this thought. Did you feel anxious, sad, frustrated, or guilty? You can write something like, "I felt rejected and unimportant."
7. **Challenge the thought:** Now, question whether your thought is based on facts or assumptions. Ask yourself:
    - What evidence do I have that this thought is true?
    - What evidence do I have that it's false?
    - How might someone else see this situation?
    - Is there a more balanced way to think about this?
8. **Reframe the thought:** Replace the distorted thought with a more balanced, rational one. If someone has not replied yet, you can try thinking *it's possible my friend just got caught up in their day. I'll wait and see if they reply later instead of assuming the worst.*
9. **Reflect on how the reframed thought changes your feelings:** Notice if shifting your perspective helps you feel less anxious or upset. Maybe you notice that "Now I feel more patient and less insecure. I don't need to take this personally."

Why This Exercise Works

By consistently tracking and analyzing your thoughts, you start to catch distortions in real time. Over time, this practice helps retrain your brain to think in a more realistic and constructive way. You may notice certain distortions showing up repeatedly, which gives you the opportunity to challenge them more effectively.

Tracking your thoughts in a diary reveals patterns you may not have noticed before, how easily your mind jumps to conclusions, magnifies problems, or assumes the worst. Recognizing these distortions is a powerful first step, but awareness alone isn't enough.

Now that you see how cognitive distortions shape your reality, the next step is to challenge them. What if those negative thoughts aren't as true as they seem? What if you could replace them with something more balanced, more constructive? In the next chapter, you'll learn how to question and reframe your thoughts, shifting from automatic self-criticism to a mindset grounded in logic, self-compassion, and clarity.

2

CHALLENGING NEGATIVE THOUGHTS

You know that voice in your head: the one that whispers doubts, magnifies mistakes, and convinces you that you're not enough? It's sneaky, persistent, and often feels like the truth. But just because a thought enters your mind doesn't mean it's accurate or worth believing. Negative thinking can shape how you see yourself and the world, limiting your potential and stealing your joy before you even get started.

Maybe you assume the worst when plans change, or you replay awkward conversations like they define your entire character. These patterns aren't just frustrating; they create a cycle that reinforces self-doubt. But what if you could catch these thoughts before they take over? What if you could break the habit of believing every critical idea that pops into your mind?

Challenging negative thoughts isn't about ignoring them or forcing yourself to "think positive." It's about questioning them, breaking them down, and deciding whether they actually serve you because when you learn to challenge your thoughts, you take back control. You shift from being at the mercy of your mind to actively shaping it. That's where real change begins.

INTRODUCE TECHNIQUES TO QUESTION AND CHALLENGE NEGATIVE THOUGHTS

That shift from being at the mercy of your mind to actively shaping it is where real, healthy change begins. But how do you actually challenge negative thoughts when they feel so automatic, so convincing?

The key is to question them, break them down, and replace them with something more balanced.

Let's explore some powerful techniques that can help you do just that.

Catch and Label the Thought

Before you can challenge a negative thought, you have to recognize it. This means becoming aware of when your mind is feeding you a negative story. It could be subtle, like a quiet assumption that you're going to fail, or loud, like an overwhelming wave of self-criticism.

Instructions

1. The moment you notice a negative thought, pause.
2. Say to yourself (internally or out loud), "This is a negative thought."
3. If possible, write it down in a journal or notes app. Seeing it in front of you creates distance from the thought.

Why It Works

Labeling a thought helps you separate it from reality (Johnson, 2023). Instead of unconsciously accepting it as truth, you begin to see it as just that, a thought, not a fact. This small shift makes it easier to challenge and change the narrative.

Ask Yourself: Is This True?

Negative thoughts often feel like cold, hard facts, but they're usually exaggerated or based on emotions rather than reality. By questioning their accuracy, you weaken their hold.

Instructions

1. Take your negative thought and ask yourself, "Is this 100% true?"
2. Look for concrete evidence. What proof do you actually have? Would this hold up in court?
3. Ask yourself, "Would I say this to a close friend?" If not, why am I saying it to myself?
4. Consider alternative explanations. What are other possible ways to look at this situation?

For example, a negative thought can be *I completely embarrassed myself in that meeting. Everyone thinks I'm incompetent.*

You can change it by thinking:

- *Did I really embarrass myself?*
- *Did I just stumble on a word?*
- *Did everyone really think that, or is this my fear talking?*

Why It Works

This technique forces you to step back from emotional reasoning. Instead of blindly accepting a negative thought, you engage your logical brain to assess whether it's actually true.

Reframe the Thought

Once you've questioned a negative thought, you can redirect it into something more balanced. This doesn't mean forcing toxic positivity; it's about finding a more constructive perspective.

Instructions

1. Identify the negative thought you want to reframe.
2. Challenge its accuracy (using the previous technique).
3. Replace it with a more balanced version.

A negative thought can be *I'm terrible at my job*. A reframed thought can be *I made a mistake today, but that doesn't mean I'm terrible at my job. I've handled plenty of things well before.*

Why It Works

Reframing helps you develop a healthier inner dialogue. It stops negativity from becoming an identity and allows you to see setbacks as temporary rather than defining (Ackerman, 2018).

The "What Would You Tell a Friend?" Technique

We tend to be much kinder to others than we are to ourselves. When negative thoughts take over, imagine a friend who is struggling with the exact same thought. What would you say to them?

Instructions

1. Picture a close friend coming to you with the same negative thought.
2. Write or say aloud how you'd respond to them.
3. Now, apply that same kindness to yourself. Your thought can be: *I'll never be successful.* However, what you'd tell your friend would change into, "That's not true at all. Success isn't instant, and you've already made progress. One setback doesn't define your entire future."

Why It Works

This technique exposes the double standard in how you treat yourself versus others. It encourages self-compassion, which is essential for overcoming negative thinking.

The "5 Whys" Technique

Sometimes, negative thoughts stick because they're rooted in deeper fears or beliefs. The "5 Whys" technique helps you dig deeper and uncover the real issue.

Instructions

1. Identify a negative thought.
2. Ask yourself, "Why do I believe this?"
3. Answer that question, then ask "Why?" again.
4. Repeat this five times to get to the root of the belief.

For instance, if the negative Thought is *I'm not good enough*. Ask yourself:

- Why do I believe this? Because I never seem to do things perfectly.
- Why does that matter? Because I feel like people only respect perfection.
- Why do I think that? Because I was criticized a lot growing up.
- Why does that still affect me? Because I still tie my worth to how others see me.
- Why is that? Because I've never learned to validate myself.

Why It Works

This method helps you uncover the deeper cause behind negative thoughts, making it easier to address the real issue rather than just surface-level fears.

The Thought Replacement List

Sometimes, it helps to have go-to replacements for common negative thoughts. By preparing these in advance, you can challenge negativity more quickly.

Instructions

1. Write down three to five negative thoughts you often have. For example, you can write, "I always mess things up."
2. Next to each one, write a more balanced, realistic replacement. Now, for he above example, the replacement

thought would be, "I make mistakes sometimes, but so does everyone. It doesn't define me."
3. Keep this list handy and refer to it when needed.

Why It Works

This technique helps create new mental pathways over time. The more you replace negative thoughts with balanced ones, the more automatic it becomes.

Create a Mental "Stop" Signal

Sometimes, negative thoughts spiral out of control. A mental stop signal can help interrupt the cycle before it takes over.

Instructions

1. Choose a short phrase or image that represents stopping (e.g., "Stop," "Not today," or a stop sign).
2. When you catch a negative spiral, visualize or say this cue.
3. Immediately redirect your focus to something else—deep breathing, a physical movement, or a new thought.

Why It Works

This technique disrupts negativity before it gains momentum. Over time, your brain learns to stop these thought spirals earlier.

Evidence Journaling

Keeping track of evidence against your negative thoughts can help shift your mindset over time.

Instructions

1. Each day, write down one piece of evidence that contradicts a negative thought you've had.
2. Over time, review these entries to reinforce a more balanced mindset.

Why It Works

Your brain tends to focus on what you feed it (Smoul, 2025). The more evidence you gather against negative beliefs, the weaker they become.

These techniques won't silence negative thoughts overnight, but they will help you weaken their grip. The more you practice questioning and replacing them, the more control you take back.

THE IMPORTANCE OF EVIDENCE-BASED THINKING

Each time you challenge a negative thought, you prove to yourself that you don't have to believe everything your mind tells you. But to truly break free from negativity, you need to go one step further; you need to anchor your thinking in reality. This is where evidence-based thinking comes in. Instead of letting emotions dictate your beliefs, you shift to a mindset that values facts over assumptions, proof over perception.

Why Evidence-Based Thinking Matters

Your mind is powerful, but it's not always accurate. It jumps to conclusions, fills in gaps, and distorts reality based on past experiences, fears, and insecurities. Negative thoughts flourish in this distorted space. If left unchecked, they can shape your entire worldview, convincing you that you're incapable, unworthy, or doomed to fail, even when reality says otherwise.

Evidence-based thinking helps you see situations as they are, rather than how your emotions interpret them. It allows you to challenge irrational fears, break harmful thought patterns, and develop a mindset that's grounded in truth. Do not mistake them as ignoring emotions. Instead, they're valuable and valid, but you are not letting them run the show without checking the facts first (Madeson, 2025).

Let's explore how you can integrate evidence-based thinking into your daily life.

Separate Feelings From Facts

Negative thoughts often feel like the truth because emotions are powerful. But just because you feel something doesn't mean it's objectively real. Learning to separate feelings from facts is the first step in adopting an evidence-based mindset.

Instructions

1. The next time you have a negative thought, pause and ask yourself: "Is this a fact," or "is this how I feel?
   - For example, if you think, *I feel like no one likes me,* recognize that this is based on emotion, not necessarily reality.
2. If it's based on feelings, take a step back and look for actual evidence. What proof supports this thought?
   - Maybe a friend just texted you yesterday to check in, or a coworker invited you to lunch; both are clear signs that people care about you.
3. Consider alternative explanations. Are there facts that contradict this thought?
   - Your mind might say, *They were just being polite,* but a more balanced view would acknowledge that people don't consistently reach out unless they genuinely care.

Why It Works

Emotions can cloud judgment. By consciously distinguishing between feelings and facts, you avoid making decisions or forming beliefs based on distorted perceptions.

Demand Proof Before Accepting a Thought

Your brain presents thoughts constantly, but not all of them deserve belief. Instead of accepting every thought as truth, train yourself to ask, "Where's the proof?"

Instructions

1. Each time you have a negative thought, challenge it with: "What actual evidence supports this?
   - If you feel "No one ever listens to me," ask yourself: "Have there been moments when someone valued your opinion, like a coworker asking for advice or a friend remembering something you said?"
2. Watch for exaggerations like always, never, everyone, no one. These words usually signal distorted thinking.
   - You may have failed at something recently, but have you ever succeeded at anything? Perhaps you successfully learned how to drive, completed a major project, or built meaningful relationships—clear counter-evidence.
3. Look for examples that contradict your thought and acknowledge them.
   - Instead of "I'll never be successful," say, "Success takes time, and I'm making progress toward my goals."

Why It Works

Negative thinking often involves broad, distorted generalizations. By demanding proof, you shift from emotional reasoning to logical analysis, weakening the negativity's grip (Goldminz, 2018).

Use the "Courtroom Test"

Imagine your thoughts are on trial. Would they hold up in a court of law? Would a judge or jury agree with your assumptions, or would they need solid evidence?

Instructions

1. When you catch yourself thinking negatively, act as a judge. "Does this thought have enough solid evidence to be considered true?"
   - If you think *I'm terrible at my job,* put that claim to the test.

2. Examine the actual proof. Have you received feedback that supports this belief?
   - Maybe you successfully met your deadlines last month, received positive comments from your boss, or improved your skills over time.
3. If the evidence is weak, rewrite the thought in a more factual, balanced way.

Why It Works

This technique forces you to approach your thoughts from a neutral, logical perspective rather than letting emotions dictate what you believe.

Track Your Thinking Patterns

Sometimes, you don't realize how often negative thinking distorts your view until you see it on paper. Keeping track of your thoughts can help you identify patterns and challenge them effectively.

Instructions

1. Keep a small notebook or use a notes app to record negative thoughts throughout the day.
   - If you find yourself thinking, *My friend didn't respond to my text. She must be mad at me;* write it down.
2. Next to each thought, note the trigger and your emotional response.
   - **Trigger:** Sent a message and didn't get an immediate reply.
   - **Emotion:** Anxiety, insecurity.
3. Review the facts. Has your friend taken longer to respond before? Could they simply be busy?
   - In reality, your friend has a demanding job and has previously taken time to respond without being upset.
4. Look for recurring patterns in your thinking. Do certain situations consistently trigger the same distorted thoughts?

Why It Works

Seeing your thoughts written out makes them easier to analyze. Over time, this practice asks your brain to automatically question negativity instead of accepting it (Thompson, 2020).

Test Your Assumptions in Real Life

Negative thoughts often predict worst-case scenarios that never actually happen. The best way to prove them wrong? Test them in real life.

Instructions

1. Identify a fear-based negative thought.
    - If you believe, "If I express my feelings, my partner will think I'm too needy," recognize that this is an assumption.
2. Instead of avoiding the situation, challenge yourself to face it.
    - The next time you feel upset or need reassurance, openly share your feelings with your partner.
3. Observe what actually happens. Did they react negatively, or was your fear unfounded?
    - Maybe they listen, offer support, and appreciate your honesty—proving your assumption wrong.

Why It Works

Fear-based thinking prospers on avoidance (Hofmann & Hay, 2018). By actively testing your assumptions, you gather real-life evidence that contradicts your negative beliefs, weakening their influence.

Get an Outside Perspective

Sometimes, you're too close to your own thoughts to see them clearly. Talking to someone you trust can help provide an objective reality check.

Instructions

1. When you're stuck in a negative thought, reach out to a trusted friend, mentor, or therapist.
   - If you're thinking, *I completely messed up that presentation. Everyone must think I'm incompetent.* Talk it through with someone.
2. Share what you're thinking and ask, "Does this sound accurate to you?"
   - Your friend might respond, "You stumbled for a second, but overall, your points were strong. No one was judging you."
3. Compare their perspective with your own perception.
   - Often, others see you more kindly than you see yourself, helping you adopt a more balanced view.

Why It Works

An outside perspective can help you see things more clearly. Others often view you more kindly than you view yourself, which can help shift your mindset.

Exercise: Triple Column Technique

This exercise helps you break free from negative thought patterns by identifying distortions and replacing them with a more balanced perspective.

Instructions

1. Divide a page into three columns:
   - **Column 1—Negative thought:** Write down the self-defeating thought.
   - **Column 2—Cognitive distortion:** Identify the thinking trap (e.g., all-or-nothing thinking, mind reading, catastrophizing).
   - **Column 3—Reframed thought:** Rewrite the thought in a balanced, positive way.

Example Table:

Negative thought	Cognitive distortion	Reframed thought
"I always ruin relationships."	Overgeneralization	"I've had challenges in some relationships, but I've also had meaningful connections and learned from my experiences."
"If I express my feelings, my partner will think I'm too needy."	Mind Reading	"I can't assume what my partner thinks. Honest communication can strengthen our relationship."
"No one cares about me."	Emotional Reasoning	"I feel lonely right now, but I have friends and family who care about me, even if they're not reaching out at this moment."
"I failed this project, so I'm a failure."	Labeling	"I struggled with this project, but that doesn't define my worth. I can learn and improve for next time."

Why It Works

This method helps you identify distorted thinking, recognize patterns, and retrain your brain to adopt a more constructive mindset (Belmont, 2017). Over time, challenging these thoughts becomes second nature, leading to a more positive and realistic outlook.

By challenging your thoughts with evidence and alternative perspectives, you create space for healthier, more rational thinking. Over time, this practice rewires your brain, making positive thinking more natural and automatic. But changing thought patterns isn't just about questioning negativity; it's also about deliberately shifting focus toward what's good. Gratitude is one of the most effective tools for reshaping your mindset, and in the next chapter, you'll discover how the simple act of appreciation can change your brain, improve resilience, and bring more joy into your daily life.

3

DEVELOPING A GRATITUDE PRACTICE

You're lying in bed, staring at the ceiling, running through a mental checklist of everything that went wrong today. Maybe you snapped at a coworker. Maybe a friend didn't text back. Maybe you just feel like you're not measuring up again. The weight of self-doubt and negativity presses in, making it hard to see anything good.

Now, imagine pressing pause on that moment for just a moment. Instead of replaying what went wrong, you shift your focus: the warmth of your blanket, the kindness of a stranger who held the door for you, and the way your coffee tasted this morning. Small things, maybe. But at that moment, something shifts. The heaviness lifts, even if just a little.

Gratitude isn't about ignoring struggles or pretending everything is perfect. It's about retraining your mind to notice what's good, even in the midst of challenges. Right now, your brain may be wired to scan for what's missing, what's lacking, and what's wrong. But gratitude? It's the tool that can help rewire that instinct. It's not just a feel-good practice—it's a mindset shift, one that can change the way you see yourself, your life, and the world around you.

HOW GRATITUDE SHIFTS FOCUS FROM NEGATIVITY TO APPRECIATION

Gratitude works like a spotlight. Whatever you shine it on becomes clearer, more vivid, more present. When negativity and self-doubt dominate your thoughts, know that's where your attention lives: on the mistakes, the shortcomings, the things that didn't go your way. But when you shift that focus toward appreciation, your perspective starts to change. It's not about denying reality or ignoring challenges; it's about broadening your view so that you see the good alongside the struggles (Jayasinghe, 2024).

How often do you automatically notice what's wrong instead of what's right?

Maybe you receive a compliment, but you brush it off, focusing instead on something you could have done better. Or you finish a project at work, but instead of feeling accomplished, you fixate on the one minor detail that wasn't perfect. This negativity bias is wired into your brain as a survival mechanism, but in everyday life, it can create a cycle of self-doubt and dissatisfaction. Gratitude interrupts that cycle by giving you a different focal point.

When you actively practice gratitude, you train your mind to recognize moments of goodness that would otherwise go unnoticed. It could be something big, like getting a promotion, or something small, like the way the sunlight hits your window in the morning. Over time, your brain becomes more attuned to these positive moments, making gratitude a natural response rather than a forced exercise. You start to feel more present, more aware of the good around you, and more capable of handling challenges without sinking into negativity (Jayasinghe, 2024).

Rewiring Your Brain for Appreciation

Neuroscience backs up what so many people have discovered firsthand: gratitude has the power to rewire your brain. When you practice gratitude regularly, it activates the brain's reward system, releasing dopamine and serotonin, neurotransmitters responsible for happiness and well-being (Chowdhury, 2019). This isn't just a temporary boost. Over time, gratitude strengthens neural pathways that make positive thinking easier and more automatic.

Let's say someone started a daily gratitude journal. At first, they might struggle to list three things they're thankful for. But after a few weeks, they begin noticing little moments throughout the day that they previously ignored: a smile from a stranger, the sound of laughter, the feeling of fresh air after being indoors. Their brain, once trained to highlight stress and shortcomings, now actively seeks out moments of joy and connection. A shift from a scarcity mindset to an abundance mindset, where appreciation replaces doubt and self-criticism.

Gratitude as a Tool for Self-Worth

If you struggle with self-doubt, gratitude can become a powerful way to reshape the way you see yourself. Often, negative thought patterns make you feel like you're not enough, not successful enough, not smart enough, or not worthy enough. But when you focus on what you do have rather than what you lack, it changes the narrative.

For example, instead of thinking, *I didn't accomplish enough today*, you might reframe it as *I made progress, and I'm grateful for the effort I put in.* Instead of dwelling on past mistakes, you might appreciate the lessons they taught you. Gratitude allows you to acknowledge your own growth, strengths, and resilience rather than fixating on perceived failures.

Finding Gratitude in Difficult Moments

One of the biggest misconceptions about gratitude is that it's only for the good times. But true gratitude is most helpful when applied during life's challenges. It doesn't mean forcing yourself to be happy in tough moments or pretending that pain doesn't exist. Instead, it means finding something to hold onto, even when things feel difficult.

Imagine you're going through a period of uncertainty, maybe a job loss, a breakup, or a time when everything feels out of your control.

It's easy to get lost in fear, frustration, or hopelessness. But gratitude can be the support that keeps you grounded. Maybe you find gratitude in the support of a friend, in the resilience you're building, or in the simple comfort of a morning routine. Even in hardship, there is always something to appreciate.

When you start making gratitude a daily habit, you'll notice something incredible: it stops feeling like an effort and starts becoming second nature. The more you practice, the more naturally your mind shifts toward appreciation, even in situations where negativity used to take over. But how do you actually integrate gratitude into your life in a way that feels meaningful and consistent? There's no one-size-fits-all approach. The key is finding gratitude practices that resonate with you, fit into your lifestyle, and, most importantly, feel authentic rather than forced.

THE SCIENCE-BACKED BENEFITS OF GRATITUDE

Research in psychology and neuroscience has repeatedly shown that practicing gratitude can improve mental health, boost resilience, and enhance overall life satisfaction (Chowdhury, 2019).

Here's a closer look at how gratitude influences the brain and body (Chowdhury, 2019; Jayasinghe, 2024):

Gratitude Improves Mental Health and Reduces Anxiety and Depression

Several studies have linked gratitude to reduced symptoms of anxiety and depression (Chowdhury, 2019). One reason for this is that gratitude reduces the production of cortisol, the stress hormone. Chronic stress and excessive cortisol levels are linked to anxiety, depression, and other mental health disorders. Gratitude also boosts dopamine and serotonin, which enhance mood and promote emotional stability.

By focusing on what's going well rather than what's going wrong, gratitude provides a natural way to lift your mood and create emotional balance.

Gratitude Increases Resilience and Emotional Strength

Life is full of challenges, but gratitude can help you navigate them with greater resilience. Research has found that grateful people are more likely to recover from setbacks, trauma, and adversity (Chowdhury, 2019).

Gratitude shifts the focus from "Why is this happening to me?" to "What can I learn from this?" or "Who has supported me through this?" This change in perspective fosters emotional strength and helps you navigate difficulties with a sense of hope rather than despair.

Gratitude Strengthens Relationships and Social Bonds

Humans are wired for connection, and gratitude plays a huge role in strengthening relationships. Expressing appreciation enhances feelings of closeness and deepens bonds with family, friends, and romantic partners.

Research has found that couples who regularly express gratitude toward each other reported higher relationship satisfaction, greater trust, and stronger emotional intimacy (Chowdhury, 2019). Additionally, showing appreciation at work improves team morale and creates a more positive workplace culture.

Simply saying "thank you" can make people feel valued, which strengthens both personal and professional relationships.

Gratitude Enhances Physical Health and Boosts Immunity

The benefits of gratitude extend beyond the mind; it also has tangible effects on physical health. A study showed that people who practiced gratitude regularly had lower blood pressure, better heart health, and stronger immune function.

The connection between gratitude and physical health may be due to its ability to reduce stress and inflammation, both of which contribute to chronic diseases. By lowering stress hormones and promoting relaxation, gratitude supports overall well-being.

DIFFERENT GRATITUDE PRACTICES

Now, you might be thinking *I understand the significance of gratitude, but how can I start practicing gratitude?*

Below are some of the most powerful gratitude practices. Each one is designed to help you break free from negative thought patterns and develop a stronger sense of self-worth. Try them out, experiment, and see which ones work best for you.

The Gratitude Letter: Expressing Deep Appreciation

The gratitude letter is an effective way to acknowledge someone who has had a positive impact on your life. It's about expressing appreciation for their kindness, support, or influence in a way you may not have before.

Instructions

1. Think of someone who has made a meaningful difference in your life. It could be a mentor, a friend, a family member, or even someone from your past.
2. Write them a letter (or an email) detailing why you appreciate them. Be specific—describe moments when they helped you, lessons they taught you, or qualities you admire about them.
3. If possible, read the letter to them in person or over the phone. If that's not feasible, simply sending it works, too.

Why It Works

Expressing gratitude outwardly deepens your sense of connection and reinforces positive emotions. Studies show that writing gratitude letters increases happiness and decreases depressive symptoms, even if you never send them (Chowdhury, 2019). It's a reminder that you're not alone and that people have shown up for you in ways that matter.

The "Three Good Things" Reflection: Shifting Perspective

This practice trains your mind to focus on positive moments by reflecting on three good things that happened each day (Chowdhury, 2019). It helps counteract negativity bias by making you more aware of the good that already exists in your life.

Instructions

1. Each night, before bed, write down three good things that happened that day.
2. They don't have to be major events—something as simple as enjoying a delicious meal, receiving a compliment, or hearing a song you love counts.
3. Take a moment to reflect on why each of these moments was meaningful.

Why It Works

Your brain naturally fixates on negative experiences more than positive ones. This practice helps balance the scale, rewiring your mind to notice and appreciate small joys. Research has shown that doing this for just two weeks can lead to greater happiness and improved mental well-being (Chowdhury, 2019).

Gratitude Walks: Engaging Your Senses

A gratitude walk is a mindful exercise where you focus on appreciating your surroundings as you move. It's a way to combine the benefits of physical movement, mindfulness, and gratitude all in one.

Instructions

1. Step outside for a walk. This can be in nature, your neighborhood, or even around your home.
2. As you walk, engage your senses. What do you see, hear, smell, and feel that you appreciate?
3. Instead of letting your mind wander, intentionally focus on

small things—maybe the warmth of the sun, the rustling of leaves, or the rhythm of your breath.

Why It Works

Movement boosts endorphins, and mindfulness enhances your ability to stay present (Perera, 2024). Combining the two with gratitude creates a powerful mood-lifting experience, helping you break free from overthinking and negative thought loops.

Gratitude Jar: A Visual Reminder of Abundance

The gratitude jar is a simple but effective way to collect and visually track the things you're grateful for over time. It's a tangible reminder of the good in your life, especially on tough days.

Instructions

1. Find a jar or container and place it somewhere visible.
2. Each day (or whenever you feel grateful), write down something you appreciate on a small piece of paper and drop it in the jar.
3. When you're feeling down or struggling with self-doubt, pull out a few notes and read them to remind yourself of all the good moments.

Why It Works

Seeing your gratitude accumulate in a physical form reinforces positive thinking (Chowdhury, 2019). This practice is especially helpful when you're feeling stuck in negativity, as it provides undeniable proof that there's always something to appreciate.

Mindful Gratitude Meditation: Deepening Appreciation

A gratitude meditation helps you slow down, focus, and cultivate appreciation in a deep and intentional way. It allows you to fully absorb feelings of gratitude rather than just acknowledge them intellectually.

Instructions

1. Find a quiet space where you won't be disturbed.
2. Close your eyes and take a few deep breaths, relaxing your body.
3. Bring to mind three things you're grateful for, one at a time. With each, visualize it clearly and immerse yourself in the feeling of appreciation.
4. Let the emotion of gratitude expand, noticing how it affects your mood and body.

Why It Works

Meditation strengthens neural pathways associated with positive emotions (Harvard Health, 2025). By repeatedly focusing on gratitude, you create a lasting shift in how you experience and process emotions, reducing stress and increasing overall well-being.

Gratitude Anchoring: Tying Gratitude to Daily Habits

This method involves linking gratitude to an existing habit so that it becomes a natural part of your routine. Instead of setting aside special time for gratitude, you integrate it seamlessly into things you already do.

Instructions

1. Choose an everyday activity, brushing your teeth, making coffee, or waiting at a stoplight.
2. Use that moment as a cue to mentally list something you're grateful for.
3. Keep it simple and consistent so that gratitude becomes second nature.

Why It Works

Habits stick better when they're tied to existing routines (Arlinghaus & Johnston, 2018). Gratitude anchoring ensures that appreciation becomes a daily practice without requiring extra effort. Over time, this small shift can create a profound impact on your mindset.

The Reverse Bucket List: Recognizing How Far You've Come

Instead of listing things you *want* to achieve, a reverse bucket list focuses on what you've *already* accomplished and experienced. It's about appreciating the journey you've taken rather than always chasing the next milestone.

Instructions

1. Take a piece of paper and write down experiences, challenges you've overcome, and personal achievements (big or small).
2. Reflect on moments when you grew, learned, or felt joy. Maybe it's a skill you mastered, a place you visited, or a fear you conquered.
3. Revisit this list when you feel stuck in self-doubt to remind yourself of your progress.

Why It Works

This practice shifts your focus from what's missing to what's already present. It builds self-worth by reinforcing the idea that you *have* achieved, learned, and grown, even if you don't always recognize it.

The Gratitude Photo Challenge: Seeing Beauty in Everyday Life

The gratitude photo challenge is a visual gratitude practice where you take photos of things you appreciate. This turns gratitude into a creative, engaging experience rather than just a mental exercise.

Instructions

1. Every day, take a photo of something that brings you joy or gratitude. It could be a sunset, a meal, a pet, or a quiet moment.
2. Keep these photos in a special album on your phone or print them out for a gratitude wall.

3. At the end of the week or month, look back and reflect on all the moments you captured.

Why It Works

This practice rewires your brain to actively search for beauty and joy in your surroundings (Chowdhury, 2019). The more you look for things to appreciate, the more your perspective shifts toward positivity.

The Gratitude Soundtrack: Music That Lifts Your Spirit

A gratitude soundtrack is a playlist that consists of songs that remind you of people, experiences, or moments you're grateful for. Music has a deep emotional connection, making this a powerful way to reinforce appreciation.

Instructions

1. Create a playlist with songs that bring back positive memories or evoke gratitude.
2. When you feel overwhelmed or discouraged, listen to this playlist as a reset.
3. If certain songs remind you of specific people, share the playlist with them and tell them why they're included.

Why It Works

Music triggers emotional memories and can instantly shift your mood (Jäncke, 2008). By tying gratitude to songs, you create an anchor that helps reinforce appreciation whenever you listen.

The Five Senses Appreciation Practice: Engaging Fully with the Present

The five senses appreciation practice is a mindful gratitude exercise that focuses on appreciating what you can see, hear, smell, taste, and touch in the moment (Camacho, 2024).

Instructions

1. Pause for a moment and list one thing you're grateful for in each of the five senses.
   - **Sight:** A beautiful color, a meaningful object, nature around you.
   - **Sound:** A favorite song, laughter, the hum of a peaceful space.
   - **Smell:** Fresh coffee, rain, a familiar scent from childhood.
   - **Taste:** A favorite meal, fresh fruit, the richness of chocolate.
   - **Touch:** Soft fabric, a warm hug, the comfort of a blanket.
2. This can be done anywhere: at home, on a walk, or in the middle of a busy day.

Why It Works

Grounding yourself in sensory appreciation helps you feel more present and reduces anxiety (Camacho, 2024). It also encourages gratitude for small, everyday pleasures that often go unnoticed.

Future Gratitude: Thanking Yourself in Advance

Future gratitude is about expressing gratitude for things before they happen by shifting your mindset from doubt to confidence, reinforcing a belief in positive outcomes.

Instructions

1. Write or say out loud: "I'm grateful for the opportunities coming my way," or "I'm thankful for the growth I'll experience through this challenge."
2. Visualize success and appreciation before it even happens.
3. This can be part of a morning routine, setting a positive tone for the day ahead.

Why It Works

Your brain doesn't always distinguish between real and imagined experiences (Gibson, 2024). Expressing gratitude in advance trains your mind to expect positive outcomes, reducing fear and hesitation.

The Gratitude Postcard Project: Spreading Positivity

The gratitude postcard project is a fun way to share gratitude by sending physical or digital postcards to people who've positively impacted your life.

Instructions

1. Get postcards or create digital ones online.
2. Write a short, heartfelt message of appreciation and mail or send them.
3. This can be for family, friends, teachers, coworkers, or even a barista who brightens your mornings.

Why It Works

This practice spreads gratitude beyond yourself. Expressing appreciation not only lifts others up but also strengthens your own sense of connection and fulfillment.

Gratitude Doodles: Turning Appreciation into Art

Instead of writing, gratitude doodles are a playful way to draw your gratitude. This creative exercise can be a fun and relaxing way to engage with appreciation.

Instructions

1. Get a notebook or tablet and sketch something you're grateful for each day.
2. It doesn't have to be perfect; simple doodles, symbols, or even colors that represent what you appreciate work just as well.
3. Over time, you'll have a visual diary of gratitude to look back on.

Why It Works

Creativity activates different parts of the brain than writing, making gratitude feel more immersive and enjoyable (Chowdhury, 2019). Plus, drawing or doodling can reduce stress and enhance mindfulness.

Gratitude Through Movement: Embodying Appreciation

Gratitude through movement is a fun way to practice gratitude physically, whether through yoga, dance, stretching, or simply mindful movement.

Instructions

1. As you move, focus on being grateful for your body's abilities, no matter what they are.
2. With each movement, say a silent *thank you* for what your body allows you to do—walking, stretching, breathing.
3. If you enjoy dancing, put on a song and move with gratitude, feeling the joy of being alive.

Why It Works

Movement releases endorphins, and when combined with gratitude, it creates a solid sense of presence and appreciation for your body, shifting focus away from self-doubt (Perera, 2024).

Developing gratitude shifts your focus from what's missing or wrong to what's abundant and meaningful in your life. However, staying present in the moment is just as important as recognizing what you're grateful for. The mind often gets caught in a cycle of past regrets or future worries, fueling stress and negativity. This is where mindfulness and meditation come in.

In the next chapter, you'll explore how training your mind to stay in the present moment can break the cycle of negative thinking, quiet mental chatter and bring a sense of calm and clarity into your life.

4

PRACTICING MINDFULNESS AND MEDITATION

Have you ever felt like your mind just won't quiet down? One moment, you're replaying an awkward conversation from years ago, and the next, you're worrying about things that haven't even happened—it's exhausting. Negative thought patterns and self-doubt can trap you in a cycle that feels impossible to break. But know that your thoughts aren't in control. *You* are.

That's where mindfulness and meditation come in. They're not just buzzwords or trendy self-care practices that have just come to life; they're devices that can quiet the mental noise and help you stay present. Instead of getting lost in worries about the future or regrets from the past, mindfulness brings you back to *right now* (Keng et al., 2011). It teaches you to observe your thoughts without letting them control you. Meditation strengthens this skill, training your mind like a muscle so you can build resilience against doubt and overthinking.

You don't have to sit cross-legged for hours to see the benefits. Even small, simple practices, like focusing on your breath during a stressful moment or truly tasting your morning coffee, can shift your mindset.

This chapter will teach you how to benefit from mindfulness and meditation practices.

HOW MINDFULNESS HELPS MANAGE NEGATIVE THOUGHTS

Think about the last time your mind spiraled into self-doubt. Maybe you made a minor mistake at work, and suddenly, your brain convinced you that you're incompetent. Or perhaps you hesitated to speak up in a conversation, and now you're replaying every awkward second, assuming everyone noticed and judged you for it. Does it sound familiar?

Negative thought patterns have a way of creeping in, multiplying, and taking control before you even realize it.

That's where mindfulness comes in. It doesn't erase negative thoughts, but it changes your relationship with them (Keng et al., 2011). Instead of getting swept away by the mental chatter, you learn to step back and *observe* it without judgment. You recognize that thoughts are just thoughts, not absolute truths.

For example, imagine you catch yourself thinking, *I'll never be good enough.* Instead of believing it and letting it dictate your mood, mindfulness helps you pause and notice, *Oh, there's that thought again.* You acknowledge it, but you don't have to accept it as reality. This simple shift takes away its power.

Studies show that mindfulness actually rewires the brain, weakening the pathways linked to anxiety and overthinking while strengthening areas responsible for focus, emotional regulation, and self-awareness (Keng et al., 2011). With consistent practice, you can train your brain to break free from habitual negative thinking.

The Power of Awareness: Recognizing Thought Patterns

Most of the time, we're so caught up in our thoughts that we don't even realize how much they control us. Mindfulness increases awareness, helping you notice patterns that fuel self-doubt and negativity (Harvard Health, 2025).

Let's say you tend to criticize yourself every time you make a mistake. You might not even be aware of how often you do it because it's become second nature. But through mindfulness, you start to catch those thoughts in real time: *There it is again—self-criticism.* With this awareness comes choice. Once you recognize a pattern, you can interrupt it.

Meditation: Training Your Mind Like a Muscle

If mindfulness is the practice of staying present, meditation is the training ground. You can think of it as going to the gym for your brain. It multiplies your ability to focus, manage emotions, and quiet self-doubt (Harvard Health, 2025).

A common misconception is that meditation requires a blank mind, but that's not the goal. Your mind *will* wander, and that's normal. The practice is in noticing when it wanders and gently bringing your focus back. Each time you do this, you strengthen the mental muscles that help you stay present and disengage from negative thoughts.

Self-Compassion: The Heart of Mindfulness

At its core, mindfulness consists of awareness and kindness. Both go hand in hand. A big part of managing negative thoughts is learning to treat yourself with the same patience and compassion you'd offer a friend.

Think about it: If a friend told you they were struggling with self-doubt, you wouldn't say, "Yeah, you're probably right—you're not good enough." But that's exactly how most people talk to themselves.

Overcoming Resistance: When Mindfulness Feels Difficult

Let's be real: mindfulness sounds simple, but in practice, it can feel frustrating. Sitting in silence with your thoughts does not always seem fun. Noticing negativity instead of pushing it away? Uncomfortable. But that discomfort is part of the process.

At first, you might feel restless, impatient, or even resistant. Your mind might tell you, *This isn't working.* But that's just another thought.

The key is to keep showing up. Over time, mindfulness becomes second nature, and the mental space it creates can be life-changing.

BASIC MEDITATION TECHNIQUES FOR AWARENESS

Meditation does not mean forcing yourself to think positively or trying to clear your mind completely. Instead, it's about developing awareness, the ability to notice your thoughts without letting them control you.

You can understand this way: Imagine sitting by a river, watching leaves float downstream. Each leaf represents a thought. Some are small and harmless, while others might be heavier, filled with doubt, worry, or regret. Without awareness, you might find yourself reaching for those heavy leaves, holding onto them, analyzing them, and letting them weigh you down. Meditation teaches you to sit back, observe, and let the leaves pass without getting caught up in them (*What Is a Floating Meditation Tank?*, 2024).

Through consistent practice, you learn that thoughts are temporary. Just because a negative thought arises doesn't mean it's true or that you have to engage with it. With time, you gain the ability to let go, creating space between you and the mental noise.

Let's explore some beginner-friendly meditation techniques that help develop this present-moment awareness.

Breath Awareness Meditation

This is one of the simplest and most effective meditation techniques. By focusing on your breath, you train your mind to stay in the present moment rather than getting caught up in worries or self-doubt (Bentley et al., 2023).

Instructions

1. Find a quiet space and sit in a comfortable position. You can sit on a cushion, a chair, or even lie down if that feels better.
2. Close your eyes or soften your gaze.

3. Take a deep breath in through your nose, feeling your belly rise. Exhale slowly through your mouth.
4. Shift your attention to your natural breathing rhythm. Notice the coolness of the air as you inhale and the warmth as you exhale.
5. If your mind starts to wander (and it will), gently bring your focus back to your breath without judgment.
6. Continue for five to ten minutes.

Why It Works

Your breath is an anchor that keeps you grounded in the present. Every time you redirect your attention back to it, you're strengthening the mental muscles that help you break free from negative thought loops.

Body Scan Meditation

This practice helps you become aware of physical sensations, release tension, and reconnect with the present moment (Scott, 2024). It's especially useful if stress or anxiety manifests in your body.

Instructions

1. Lie down or sit comfortably with your eyes closed.
2. Take a few deep breaths to settle in.
3. Begin at the top of your head, noticing any sensations—tingling, warmth, tightness.
4. Slowly move your focus down through your face, neck, shoulders, arms, hands, chest, abdomen, legs, and feet.
5. If you encounter tension, breathe into that area and allow it to soften.
6. Spend about ten to fifteen minutes scanning your body, bringing your awareness to each part.

Why It Works

Negative thoughts often come with physical tension. By directing your attention to bodily sensations, you interrupt anxious thought cycles and create a sense of relaxation (Scott, 2024).

Labeling Your Thoughts

This technique helps you step back from your thoughts instead of getting lost in them. It's particularly effective for identifying patterns of self-doubt.

Instructions

1. Sit quietly and focus on your breath for a moment.
2. As thoughts arise, mentally label them: *worrying, judging, remembering, planning.*
3. Avoid engaging with the thoughts—simply note them and return to your breath.
4. If a thought keeps returning, acknowledge it and let it pass like a cloud drifting in the sky.
5. Continue for five to ten minutes.

Why It Works

Labeling thoughts creates distance between you and your inner dialogue (Conway, 2021). Instead of identifying with every negative thought, you learn to observe them objectively.

Loving-Kindness Meditation (Metta Meditation)

This practice shifts your focus from self-criticism to self-compassion (Scott, 2020). Instead of letting negative thoughts define you, you replace them with affirming intentions.

Instructions

1. Find a quiet place and sit comfortably.
2. Take a few deep breaths to center yourself.
3. Silently repeat phrases like:

    - *"May I be happy."*
    - *"May I be healthy."*
    - *"May I be free from self-doubt."*
    - *"May I find peace."*
4. After a few minutes, extend these wishes to others—loved ones, acquaintances, and even people you struggle with.
5. Continue for ten minutes, feeling warmth and kindness radiate through you.

Why It Works

Self-doubt often stems from harsh self-judgment. This meditation rewires your mind for kindness, making it easier to treat yourself with patience and understanding (Scott, 2020).

Guided Visualization

This technique helps you replace negative thought patterns with calming mental imagery, reducing anxiety and fostering inner peace.

Instructions

1. Close your eyes and take a few deep breaths.
2. Picture yourself in a peaceful setting—perhaps a beach, a forest, or a quiet garden.
3. Engage all your senses: Feel the sun on your skin, hear the gentle waves, smell the fresh air.
4. As you immerse yourself in this scene, notice how your body and mind relax.
5. If negative thoughts arise, imagine them dissolving into the scene—like waves washing them away.
6. Continue for ten to fifteen minutes.

Why It Works

Your brain responds to mental imagery as if it were real (Pearson et al., 2015). By visualizing calmness and safety, you override stress responses and create a sense of inner stability.

Making Meditation a Daily Habit

Like any skill, meditation takes practice. You need to be consistent here and aim for progress and not perfection. Even just five minutes a day can make a difference. Try incorporating meditation into your daily routine:

- **Morning:** Set the tone for the day with breath awareness or loving-kindness meditation.
- **Midday:** Use a quick body scan or labeling technique to reset when self-doubt creeps in.
- **Evening:** Wind down with guided visualization or deep breathing before bed.

BREATHWORK: A FAST-ACTING TOOL FOR BREAKING NEGATIVE THOUGHT LOOPS

Most people think of breathing as something automatic, something that just happens. But when done intentionally, your breath becomes an effective way to break patterns of overthinking and self-doubt (Barron, 2020). By adjusting how you breathe, you can change your mental state within seconds.

Now, let's learn some highly effective methods that can help you reset your mind when negativity takes hold.

Humming Bee Breath (Bhramari Pranayama)

This technique uses vibration and sound to calm the mind and quiet intrusive thoughts. The gentle humming sound activates the vagus nerve, which plays a key role in regulating stress and emotions.

Instructions

1. Find a quiet place and sit comfortably.
2. Close your eyes and take a deep inhale through your nose.
3. As you exhale, press your lips together and make a humming sound—like a bee.
4. Feel the vibration in your face, throat, and chest.
5. Repeat for five to ten rounds, focusing on the sensation of the hum.

Why It Works

The vibrations from humming naturally slow brainwave activity, reducing stress and anxiety (Barron, 2020). This breathwork technique also shifts your focus from negative thoughts to physical sensations, helping you stay present.

5-2-5 Breath (The Thought Shifter)

This simple but effective breathing pattern helps disrupt looping thoughts and encourages mental clarity. By focusing on specific counts, you redirect your mind away from self-doubt and toward a state of calm awareness.

Instructions

1. Inhale through your nose for a count of five.
2. Hold your breath for a count of two.
3. Exhale through your nose for a count of five.
4. Repeat for several minutes, maintaining an even, steady rhythm.

Why It Works

The equal inhale and exhale create a sense of balance in the nervous system. The slight pause in the middle disrupts automatic negative thought loops, giving your brain a moment to reset (Barron, 2020).

The Physiological Sigh (Double Inhale Exhale)

This technique is based on a natural reflex that your body uses to regulate stress. It mimics the deep sighs you unconsciously take throughout the day when your body tries to reset itself.

Instructions

1. Take a deep inhale through your nose.
2. Just before you reach full capacity, take a second quick inhale to completely fill your lungs.
3. Exhale slowly and fully through your mouth with a sigh.
4. Repeat two to three times.

Why It Works

The double inhale maximizes oxygen intake and helps release built-up carbon dioxide, which reduces anxiety. This technique is incredibly effective when you're feeling overwhelmed or emotionally stuck.

The 1:2 Ratio Breath (Lengthening the Exhale)

This technique helps regulate the nervous system by extending the exhale, which signals safety to your brain. It's perfect for moments when self-doubt triggers physical tension.

Instructions

1. Inhale through your nose for a count of three.
2. Exhale slowly through your nose for a count of six.
3. Repeat, adjusting the count as needed (inhale for dour, exhale for eight).

Why It Works

Extending your exhale activates the parasympathetic nervous system, which promotes relaxation and reduces stress-related thought patterns (Bentley et al., 2023).

Tummo Breathing (Inner Fire Breath)

This Tibetan practice, made famous by extreme athletes like Wim Hof, uses rapid breathing to generate heat, improve focus, and disrupt repetitive thoughts.

Instructions

1. Sit in a comfortable position and take 30–40 quick, deep breaths through the nose.
2. On the final breath, exhale fully and hold your breath out for as long as comfortable.
3. Inhale deeply, hold for ten to fifteen seconds, and then release.
4. Repeat for three rounds.

Why It Works

Tummo breathing increases oxygen levels, which enhances mental clarity. It also builds resilience by training your mind to remain calm under controlled stress (Haghighi, 2022).

Diaphragmatic "Wave" Breathing

This technique focuses on deepening the breath into the lower belly, helping to override the stress response and shift focus away from overthinking.

Instructions

1. Place one hand on your chest and the other on your belly.
2. Inhale deeply through your nose, feeling your belly expand first, then your chest.
3. Exhale slowly through your mouth, reversing the motion—chest deflates first, then belly.
4. Repeat for a few minutes, ensuring each breath flows in a smooth, wave-like motion.

Why It Works

Diaphragmatic breathing increases oxygen flow to the brain, helping to quiet mental chatter and create a sense of stability (Bentley et al., 2023).

4-7-8 Breathing (The Relaxing Breath)

The 4-7-8 breathing technique was developed by Dr. Andrew Weil, based on ancient pranayama practices. It's often referred to as the "relaxing breath" because it promotes immediate relaxation by activating the parasympathetic nervous system. This method is especially useful for reducing anxiety, calming racing thoughts, and improving sleep (WebMD Editorial Contributors, 2023b).

Instructions

1. Sit comfortably with your back straight.
2. Close your eyes and take a deep breath in through your nose for a count of four.
3. Hold your breath for a count of seven.
4. Exhale slowly and completely through your mouth for a count of eight, making a soft "whoosh" sound.
5. Repeat this cycle for four rounds.

Why It Works

The 4-7-8 breathing technique works by slowing down your breathing, which triggers the body's relaxation response, helping you feel calmer almost instantly. Holding your breath for seven counts increases oxygen flow to the brain, grounding you and making you feel more in control. The extended exhale of eight counts signals to your nervous system that it is safe to relax, counteracting stress, overthinking, and feelings of panic (WebMD Editorial Contributors, 2023b).

Box Breathing (The Focus Enhancer)

Box breathing, also known as "square breathing," is a structured breathing technique used by athletes and mindfulness practitioners to enhance focus, reduce stress, and improve mental clarity (WebMD Editorial Contributors, 2023a). It's ideal for moments when you feel mentally scattered or overwhelmed by self-doubt.

Instructions

1. Sit comfortably and close your eyes if you'd like.
2. Inhale deeply through your nose for a count of four.
3. Hold your breath for a count of four.
4. Exhale slowly through your mouth for a count of four.
5. Hold your breath again for a count of four.
6. Repeat this cycle for four to six rounds, maintaining a steady rhythm

Why It Works

Box breathing works by slowing down your breath, which activates the body's relaxation response and helps reduce stress almost instantly. Holding the breath for seven counts increases oxygen flow to the brain, promoting a sense of calm and control, while the extended exhale of eight counts signals the nervous system to relax, reducing feelings of anxiety and overthinking (Bentley et al., 2023). By focusing on the breath count, your mind shifts away from negative thoughts, breaking the cycle of self-doubt and emotional overwhelm.

Making Breathwork a Habit

The best way to get the most out of these techniques is to practice them *before* you feel overwhelmed by negative thoughts. Here's how to integrate them into your routine:

- **Morning reset:** Start your day with 5-2-5 breathing to set a clear, calm mindset.
- **Midday reboot:** If self-doubt creeps in, use the Physiological Sigh to reset instantly.
- **Evening wind down:** Humming Bee Breath before bed can help quiet a restless mind.

The beauty of breathwork is that it's always available to you. No matter where you are or what's happening in your mind, you can always return to your breath.

Mindfulness teaches you to observe your thoughts without getting lost in them, creating distance between yourself and negativity. But awareness alone isn't enough; what you do with your time also shapes your mental state. When your days are filled with activities that bring you joy and fulfillment, there's less room for negativity to take hold.

The following chapter focuses on the importance of engaging in positive activities, from hobbies to physical movement, and how they can act as natural antidotes to stress, overthinking, and self-doubt.

5

ENGAGING IN POSITIVE ACTIVITIES

You wake up feeling drained, your mind already tangled in worries before your feet even touch the floor. It's another day of overthinking, another day of feeling stuck in the same cycle of self-doubt. You tell yourself you'll shake it off, but the weight of negativity lingers. Then, your phone buzzes. A friend invites you for a morning walk at the park. You hesitate; staying in bed feels easier, but something inside you says, just go.

As you step outside, the crisp air fills your lungs, and the gentle beat of walking starts to clear your mind. The sun filters through the trees, painting everything in a golden hue. Your friend cracks a joke, and for the first time today, you laugh, genuinely laugh. You realize something powerful: when you engage in activities that bring you joy, even the heaviest thoughts lose their grip.

Positive activities aren't just distractions; they are lifelines. Whether it's painting, hiking, cooking, or playing an instrument, immersing yourself in something uplifting shifts your focus from self-doubt to self-growth. The more you fill your life with meaningful actions, the less space negativity has to take root.

So, what's one thing you can do today to break the cycle?

Let's learn it in this chapter.

IMPORTANCE OF PARTICIPATING IN ACTIVITIES

That one walk in the park may have felt small, but it was a turning point. For the first time in a while, you felt lighter, more present. It wasn't magic; just movement, fresh air, and connection. Yet, it made a difference. This is the strength of engaging in positive activities: they shift your focus, help you break free from overthinking, and remind you that joy does not translate to something you have to wait for. Instead, it's something you create.

When your mind is filled with negative thoughts, it's easy to withdraw from life. You tell yourself you'll feel better once your problems are solved, once your confidence returns, once things change. But waiting for the perfect moment keeps you stuck. The real shift happens when you actively engage in experiences that bring joy and fulfillment, no matter how small they seem.

Why Positive Activities Matter

Have you ever noticed how time seems to slow down when you're absorbed in something you love?

Maybe it's painting, where each brushstroke feels like a conversation between your emotions and the canvas. Or maybe it's dancing, where the music drowns out your doubts, and for those few minutes, nothing else matters. When you engage in activities that spark joy, your brain releases dopamine and serotonin, which enhance your mood and counteract stress (Kop et al., 2011). So, they turn away from being a distraction to rewiring your mind for positivity.

Beyond the science, these activities give you a sense of purpose. When self-doubt spreads in your mind, it often convinces you that you're not good enough or that nothing you do matters. But when you lose yourself in a meaningful activity, you prove to yourself that you are capable, that you can create, and that you do have something valuable to contribute.

Finding Your Flow

Not all activities have the same impact. Scrolling through social media or binge-watching TV might seem like easy ways to escape negative thoughts, but they often leave you feeling worse. The goal is to engage in something that makes you feel alive.

This is where the concept of "flow" comes in. Flow happens when you're so deeply immersed in an activity that time fades away. Psychologist Mihaly Csikszentmihalyi, who coined the term, found that people are happiest when they're in this state (Oppland, 2016). Be it writing, rock climbing, knitting, or playing chess, finding your flow takes you out of your worries and into the present moment. It gives you momentum, a feeling that you can move forward, that you *can* create something meaningful.

If you're not sure what activities bring you joy, experiment. Try new things. Join a dance class, take up photography, start a journal, or learn how to make homemade candles. The point isn't to be perfect at it; it's to *do* it.

The Social Connection Factor

Some activities are effective because they connect you with others. When self-doubt takes over, isolation often follows. You convince yourself that no one understands, that you're better off alone. However, research shows that social engagement is one of the strongest ways to boost emotional well-being (Wickramaratne et al., 2022).

Think about the last time you shared a laugh with a friend or worked on a project with someone. Human connection has a way of lifting the fog of negativity. Even volunteering, where you focus on helping others, can be a game-changer. It shifts your perspective, reminding you that you have something valuable to offer.

Turning Small Actions into Lasting Habits

The key to making positive activities work for you isn't just doing them once; it's making them a part of your routine. It doesn't have to be overwhelming. Start small. Set aside just 10 minutes a day for something that brings you joy. It can be journaling, sketching, or playing a musical instrument. Over time, those small moments add up, and before you know it, you've built a life where pleasure is a habit, not an afterthought.

The Science Behind Movement and Mood

Exercise does not translate to just about getting fit; it's about getting free. Free from stress, free from anxious thoughts, and free from the weight of negativity. Even a short 10-minute walk can increase dopamine and serotonin levels, helping to reduce feelings of anxiety and self-doubt.

Beyond brain chemistry, movement also reduces levels of cortisol, the stress hormone. If you've ever felt like your thoughts were racing uncontrollably, exercise helps regulate your nervous system, bringing you back to a state of calm. Studies show that regular physical activity can be as effective as medication in reducing symptoms of depression and anxiety (Wickramaratne et al., 2022).

HOW HOBBIES AND INTERESTS CAN COUNTERACT NEGATIVE THINKING

Movement reminds you that you are strong, that you can take action, and that even when your mind feels heavy, your body is capable of pushing forward. But physical activity isn't the only way to shift your mindset. Engaging in hobbies and personal interests can be just as powerful.

When negative thoughts take over, they create a loop of self-doubt and overanalysis. Your mind fixates on what's wrong, what could go wrong, and why you're not good enough. Hobbies disrupt that cycle. They give you something to focus on that's outside of your worries. They engage your hands, your mind, and your creativity in ways that promote growth and fulfillment. Most importantly, they remind you that you are capable of joy.

Hobbies provide structure, challenge, and a sense of accomplishment, all of which help counteract self-doubt (Arlinghaus & Johnston, 2018). Unlike passive distractions (like mindlessly scrolling on your phone), hobbies require active engagement, which shifts your focus away from negative thoughts and into the present moment.

Here are some hobbies that are particularly effective for rewiring your mind and instructions on how to get started:

Journaling: Rewriting Your Inner Narrative

Writing down your thoughts helps you process emotions, recognize negative patterns, and reframe your mindset. Whether you prefer free writing, gratitude journaling, or structured prompts, this practice turns self-reflection into a tool for self-improvement.

Instructions

1. Grab a notebook or open a digital document.
2. Start with five minutes a day, writing anything that comes to mind.
3. If you're stuck, try prompts like:
   - "What's one thing that went well today?"
   - "What's something I'm grateful for?"
4. Avoid overanalyzing. This is for you, not for perfection.

Why It Works

Journaling helps you gain clarity, recognize recurring negative thoughts, and create a healthier perspective on challenges. Studies show that expressive writing reduces stress and improves emotional regulation (Niles et al., 2013).

Painting or Drawing: Translating Feelings into Colors

Art is a form of emotional expression that doesn't require words. Be it painting, sketching, or even adult coloring books, creating art allows you to externalize your thoughts and emotions.

Instructions

1. Get a simple sketchpad and colored pencils or a paint set and canvas.
2. Set aside 10–15 minutes to doodle or paint freely—no rules, no pressure.
3. Try expressing your emotions through color (e.g., calming blues for peace, fiery reds for passion).

Why It Works

Engaging in art activates the brain's creative centers, reducing stress and promoting mindfulness. It shifts your focus from internal worries to external expression, giving your mind a break from negative loops (Martin et al., 2018).

Gardening: Cultivating Growth and Patience

Tending to plants (whether a full garden or a single potted plant) can be a grounding and therapeutic activity. Gardening teaches patience, responsibility, and appreciation for small progress.

Instructions

1. Start with easy-to-care-for plants like succulents, herbs, or flowers.
2. Spend a few minutes each day watering, pruning, or simply observing them.
3. Try growing something from a seed to witness its transformation.

Why It Works

Caring for plants mirrors the process of personal growth. Just as plants need time, attention, and nourishment, so do you. Plus, research shows that interacting with nature reduces cortisol levels and promotes relaxation (Jimenez, 2021).

Playing an Instrument: Turning Thoughts Into Sound

Music has a direct impact on emotions. Learning to play an instrument, even at a beginner level, can provide a sense of achievement while acting as an emotional outlet.

Instructions

1. Choose an instrument that interests you (keyboard, guitar, ukulele, or even drumming on household objects).
2. Start with simple lessons on YouTube or beginner-friendly apps.
3. Play for fun—don't stress about sounding perfect.

Why It Works

Music engages multiple areas of the brain, improving cognitive function and emotional regulation. It provides a structured yet creative way to channel energy and emotions (Jäncke, 2008).

Cooking or Baking: Creating Something Nourishing

Cooking is a hands-on, sensory-rich activity that requires focus and creativity. Whether you're preparing a simple meal or trying a new recipe, it gives a sense of accomplishment.

Instructions

1. Pick a recipe that excites you.
2. Gather ingredients and focus on the process: smelling, tasting, and appreciate the experience.
3. Experiment with flavors and presentation, making it fun rather than a chore.

Why It Works

Cooking provides instant gratification and a tangible outcome, reinforcing the idea that effort leads to results. It also encourages mindfulness as you engage with textures, aromas, and flavors.

Photography: Capturing Moments of Beauty

Photography encourages you to see the world differently. Instead of focusing on worries, it shifts your attention to details: light, texture, and composition.

Instructions

1. Use your phone camera or a simple digital camera.
2. Go outside and take photos of things that catch your eye—flowers, cityscapes, candid moments.
3. Challenge yourself with themes like capturing "happiness" in everyday life.

Why It Works

Photography trains your mind to seek beauty and meaning in your surroundings. It shifts your perspective from what's wrong to what's worth capturing.

Learning a New Skill: Challenging Your Mindset

When you're stuck in negative thinking, learning something new provides a refreshing sense of progress. Whether it's coding, knitting, or a new language, acquiring skills fosters confidence.

Instructions

1. Choose something you've always been curious about.
2. Find free online resources (YouTube, apps, or local classes).
3. Set small, achievable goals to track progress.

Why It Works

Learning challenges the belief that you're "not good enough." With every bit of progress, you prove to yourself that growth is possible.

The best part about hobbies is that they're always available. They don't require a perfect mood or the right circumstances. You can start anytime. The more you engage in activities that bring you delight and fulfillment, the more you train your mind to focus on what's possible rather than what's wrong.

Activity Scheduling for a Positive Mindset

To make engaging in positive activities a habit, you're going to create a personalized activity schedule—a simple, structured way to ensure that each day includes at least one enjoyable activity. This isn't about adding more to your to-do list or feeling pressured to be productive. It's about carving out time for joy and intentionally shifting your energy toward what uplifts you.

Step 1: Identify Your Enjoyable Activities

Start by listing activities that bring you joy, fulfillment, or relaxation. These can be hobbies, physical activities, social interactions, or simple pleasures. The key is to choose things that genuinely make you feel good.

Here are some ideas to get you started:

- **Creative activities:** painting, journaling, playing an instrument, photography
- **Physical activities:** walking, yoga, cycling, dancing
- **Social activities:** calling a friend, having coffee with someone, joining a club
- **Mindfulness activities:** meditation, deep breathing, listening to calming music
- **Simple pleasures:** watching a sunset, reading a book, playing with a pet

Take a few moments to jot down at least five activities that resonate with you.

Step 2: Plan Your Daily Activity

Now that you have your list, it's time to incorporate these activities into your daily routine. The best way to do this is by choosing one enjoyable activity per day and scheduling it like an appointment with yourself.

Here's a sample template you can use:

Day	Activity	Time	Notes
Monday	Morning walk in the park	7:30 a.m.	Start the day with fresh air and movement
Tuesday	Call a friend for a casual chat	6:00 p.m.	Strengthen social connection
Wednesday	Try a new recipe for dinner	8:00 p.m.	Engage in creativity and nourishment
Thursday	Journal for 10 minutes	9:00 p.m.	Reflect and process emotions
Friday	Listen to music and dance around the house	5:30 p.m.	Release tension and uplift mood
Saturday	Visit a local café and read a book	2:00 p.m.	Enjoy a peaceful solo outing
Sunday	Practice meditation for 15 minutes	8:00 a.m.	Start the day with calm and clarity

Your schedule doesn't have to be rigid. The goal is to make enjoyable activities an intentional part of your day. You can modify the times based on your routine, but commit to engaging in at least *one* uplifting activity each day.

Step 3: Set Reminders and Remove Barriers

One of the biggest reasons people skip enjoyable activities is simply forgetting or feeling "too busy." To stay on track:

- Set reminders on your phone or write activities in your planner.
- Keep supplies handy (place your journal on your nightstand or set out workout clothes the night before).

- Make it easy. If an activity feels like too much effort, start small (instead of a 30-minute workout, do 5 minutes).

Step 4: Track How You Feel

As you engage in your daily activities, take a moment to reflect on how they impact your mood. Did the activity make you feel lighter? More energized? Less stressed? Keeping a simple log of your experiences can help you see the benefits more clearly and stay motivated to continue.

Use this format:

Date	Activity	Mood before	Mood after	Notes
March 18	Morning walk	Tired, anxious	Refreshed, calmer	Loved the fresh air
March 19	Journaling	Stressed, overthinking	Clear-headed, relaxed	Helped me process emotions
March 20	Called a friend	Lonely, unmotivated	Happy, connected	Great conversation

Not every activity will have a dramatic effect, and that's okay. The goal is progress, not perfection. The more consistently you engage in positive activities, the more you'll notice small but meaningful shifts in your mindset.

Why This Works

Engaging in pleasurable activities increases dopamine production, which enhances motivation and well-being (Martin et al., 2018). Additionally, when you intentionally plan enjoyable moments, you shift your focus away from stressors and into active self-care.

Joyful activities are more than just distractions; they actively reinforce positive emotions and counteract negativity. But even as you engage in uplifting experiences, your relationship with yourself plays a good role in your mental well-being. Negative self-talk and perfectionism can erode even the strongest foundations of positivity. That's why self-compassion is essential. In the next chapter, you'll learn how to replace self-criticism with kindness, let go of unrealistic expectations, and treat yourself with the same patience and understanding you would offer to a close friend.

6

BUILDING SELF-COMPASSION

When was the last time you spoke kindly to yourself? Not just a passing thought, but a real moment of self-encouragement, like telling yourself, *You're doing your best, and that's enough*? If you're like most people struggling with self-doubt, chances are, you extend more patience, empathy, and forgiveness to others than you do to yourself.

Self-compassion isn't about letting yourself off the hook or avoiding responsibility; it's about treating yourself with the same kindness and understanding that you'd offer a close friend.

The good news is that you can change that voice. You can learn to replace self-criticism with self-acceptance, perfectionism with patience, and guilt with grace. The more you practice self-compassion, the more resilient, confident, and emotionally balanced you become. It's time to rewrite the way you speak to yourself, and that starts now.

WHAT IS SELF-COMPASSION?

If changing the way you speak to yourself is the first step, then understanding what self-compassion truly means is the next. You might have heard the term before, but have you ever stopped to think about what it looks like in practice?

Self-compassion is the ability to treat yourself with kindness, understanding, and patience, especially when you're struggling, feeling inadequate, or facing failure. It's about replacing self-judgment with self-acceptance and recognizing that imperfection is part of being human. Dr. Kristin Neff, one of the leading researchers on self-compassion, defines it as having three key components (Neff, 2009):

1. **Self-kindness vs. self-judgment:** Speaking to yourself with warmth and encouragement rather than harsh criticism.
2. **Common humanity vs. isolation:** Understanding that everyone struggles, fails, and experiences pain, not just you.
3. **Mindfulness vs. over-identification:** Acknowledging negative thoughts and emotions without letting them consume or define you.

In other words, self-compassion means recognizing your pain, treating yourself with the same care you'd give a loved one, and choosing to move forward with gentleness rather than self-blame.

The Role of Self-Compassion in Overcoming Negative Thoughts

Negative thoughts can be relentless. They come in when you least expect them, whispering doubts, replaying past mistakes, and convincing you that you're not good enough. If you don't address them, they can spiral into deeper self-doubt, anxiety, or even depression.

This is where self-compassion becomes an effective way. It doesn't stop negative thoughts from appearing, but it changes how you respond to them. Instead of getting trapped in a cycle of self-criticism, self-compassion allows you to acknowledge your struggles while also offering yourself support.

Imagine you've made a mistake at work. Your inner critic might say, *You're so careless. You always mess things up.* But self-compassion shifts the narrative: *That was a mistake, but mistakes happen. I can learn from this and do better next time.* This small but deep shift makes a huge difference in how you process setbacks.

Here's how self-compassion actively helps you break free from negative thought patterns:

Reduces Self-Criticism and Harsh Inner Dialogue

Your inner critic can be loud and unforgiving, constantly pointing out flaws and shortcomings. Self-compassion softens this voice by introducing kindness and perspective. Instead of berating yourself for not being "good enough," you learn to acknowledge your efforts and recognize that perfection is an impossible standard.

Breaks the Cycle of Overthinking

When negative thoughts take over, it's easy to spiral into overthinking, rehashing past mistakes, obsessing over what you should have done, and imagining worst-case scenarios. Self-compassion interrupts this cycle by encouraging mindfulness. You acknowledge the thought without attaching unnecessary judgment or exaggeration to it.

Encourages Emotional Resilience

Self-compassion builds resilience by helping you handle setbacks with grace. Instead of seeing failure as a reflection of your worth, you begin to see it as a natural part of growth. This allows you to recover from disappointments faster and move forward with confidence.

Strengthens Self-Worth and Self-Acceptance

One of the biggest struggles with negative thoughts is that they chip away at your self-worth. You start believing that you are only as valuable as your achievements, appearance, or other external factors. Self-compassion helps you see that your worth isn't conditional; it exists simply because you *are*.

Helps You Handle Difficult Emotions With Care

Negative thoughts often come with difficult emotions like shame, guilt, or sadness. When you lack self-compassion, you might suppress these emotions or judge yourself for feeling them. But with self-compassion, you allow yourself to feel emotions without letting them define you.

PRACTICES TO CULTIVATE KINDNESS TOWARD ONESELF

Self-compassion isn't just a concept; it's a practice. It's not something you either have or don't have; it's something you develop over time through intentional actions. You already know that speaking kindly to yourself, reframing negative thoughts, and acknowledging your struggles without self-judgment are key steps. But how do you truly integrate self-compassion into your daily life?

Many people rely on common strategies like affirmations, journaling, or mindfulness meditation. While these are helpful, there are also unique and lesser-known practices that can be just as—if not more—effective. These practices work because they tap into different aspects of your brain and emotions, making self-compassion feel more natural and deeply ingrained.

The Self-Compassion Break—But With a Twist

The Self-Compassion Break is a well-known exercise developed by Dr. Kristin Neff (Neff, 2009). It involves pausing in moments of distress and practicing three key steps:

1. Acknowledge that you're struggling (*"This is a difficult moment."*)
2. Recognize that struggle is part of being human (*"I'm not alone in this."*)
3. Offer yourself kindness (*"May I be gentle with myself right now."*)

But here's the twist: Instead of just thinking these words, engage your senses to reinforce them.

Instructions

1. **Touch:** Place a hand on your chest, give yourself a gentle hug, or squeeze your arm. Physical touch can trigger the release of oxytocin, the "bonding hormone," which calms your nervous system.
2. **Sound:** Instead of just saying kind words in your head, whisper them or hum a soothing tune to yourself. The vibrations of your voice can be deeply calming.
3. **Sight:** Look at a photo of yourself as a child and speak those words of kindness directly to that younger version of you. This helps bypass your inner critic and taps into your instinct to nurture.

Why It Works

Activating your senses grounds you in the present and makes self-compassion a full-body experience (Neff, 2009).. It shifts self-kindness from an abstract idea into something tangible and deeply felt.

Writing a Self-Compassion Permission Slip

Many people hold themselves to impossibly high standards, expecting perfection and productivity at all times. If you're used to being hard on yourself, you might struggle with allowing rest, mistakes, or even joy. A self-compassion permission slip can help.

Instructions

1. Write yourself a literal permission slip as if you were a teacher or boss granting you time off.
2. Use specific wording based on what you need:
    - "I give myself permission to take a break when I feel overwhelmed."
    - "I give myself permission to not be perfect today."
    - "I give myself permission to set boundaries without guilt."

3. Keep it somewhere visible (on your desk, in your wallet, as a phone wallpaper) and read it when you start feeling self-critical.

Why It Works

Your brain responds to written commitments differently than fleeting thoughts (Thompson, 2020). Seeing your own words granting yourself kindness helps override deep-seated guilt or self-imposed pressure.

The "Compassion Jar" Practice

A gratitude jar is a common tool, but a Compassion Jar takes it a step further by focusing on self-love rather than external gratitude.

Instructions

1. Find a jar or box and small slips of paper.
2. Every day, write down one act of self-compassion you practiced or one kind thing you wish someone would say to you.
3. When you're feeling self-doubt or negativity creeping in, pull a note from the jar and read it aloud.

Why It Works

This practice builds a backlog of kindness that you can draw upon in difficult moments. Instead of relying on motivation to be kind to yourself, you create a system where self-compassion becomes a daily habit.

The Reverse Apology Exercise

Most people apologize too much for things that don't require an apology, taking up space, setting boundaries, and needing rest. This practice flips that instinct on its head by replacing unnecessary apologies with self-compassion.

Instructions

1. The next time you catch yourself saying, *I'm sorry for being emotional,* replace it with, *Thank you for understanding that I have feelings.*
2. Instead of saying, "I'm sorry, I need a break," say, "I appreciate myself for recognizing when I need rest."
3. Instead of saying, "I'm sorry for talking too much," say, "I value my thoughts and my right to express them."

Why It Works

Apologizing unnecessarily reinforces self-judgment. By shifting to appreciation instead, you train your mind to see your needs and emotions as valid rather than burdensome.

Mirror Work: Talking to Your Reflection With Kindness

Many people struggle with self-compassion because they are disconnected from themselves. Looking into a mirror and speaking directly to yourself can feel uncomfortable at first, but it's one of the fastest ways to build self-acceptance.

Instructions

1. Stand in front of a mirror, make eye contact with yourself, and say a few kind sentences aloud. Start with something simple:
    - "I see you, and I appreciate you."
    - "You are doing your best, and that is enough."
    - "You don't have to be perfect to be worthy of love."
2. If this feels too vulnerable, start by simply placing a hand on your heart while looking at your reflection.

Why It Works

Eye contact activates the brain's social bonding responses (Luft et al., 2022). When you look into your own eyes with kindness, you start forming a healthier, more compassionate relationship with yourself.

Self-Compassion Through Music Therapy

Music has a direct impact on emotions, but most people only use it passively. Instead of just listening to songs, use music intentionally as a tool for self-kindness.

Instructions

1. Create a self-compassion playlist filled with songs that make you feel safe, understood, or uplifted.
2. Sing to yourself, even if you think you have a terrible voice. The vibrations from singing activate the vagus nerve, which calms your nervous system.
3. Write yourself a song or rewrite the lyrics of a familiar tune with words of kindness.

Why It Works

Music has a unique ability to bypass logical resistance and speak directly to emotions (Jäncke, 2008). By using it intentionally, you create an environment that naturally nurtures self-compassion.

The Five-Year-Old Test

If you're struggling with a mistake, negative thought, or harsh self-judgment, try applying the Five-Year-Old Test.

Instructions

1. Imagine that a five-year-old child made the same mistake or was feeling the same way you are now.
2. How would you respond to them? What words of comfort would you offer?
3. Now, apply that same level of kindness to yourself.

Why It Works

When we externalize our struggles, it's easier to see how unreasonable our self-judgment is. Treating yourself with the kindness you'd give a child helps shift your perspective from criticism to care.

Self-compassion is like a muscle—the more you practice it, the stronger it becomes. You've already explored some unique ways to nurture kindness toward yourself, but there's always room to expand your toolkit. Since self-doubt and negative thinking can be deeply ingrained, using a variety of approaches helps ensure that self-compassion becomes second nature.

"Dear Future Me" Letters

Sometimes, the person who needs to hear the most compassion from you is *future you*. Writing letters to yourself (especially during difficult times)can provide you with support and encouragement when you need it most.

Instructions

1. Think about an upcoming event that might trigger stress or self-doubt (a job interview, a difficult conversation, a personal challenge).
2. Write yourself a letter as if you were comforting a close friend:
    - Acknowledge your fears.
    - Offer reassurance.
    - Remind yourself of past strengths and resilience.
3. Seal the letter in an envelope or schedule it to be emailed to yourself on the day you'll need it most.

Why It Works

It allows you to be your own support system. When self-doubt inevitably appears, you'll have a reminder from a kinder, more rational version of yourself.

"What Would My Best Friend Say?" Exercise

Your inner critic often says things you would *never* say to someone you love. This exercise helps you counteract negative self-talk by imagining how a supportive person would respond.

Instructions

1. The next time you catch yourself in self-criticism, pause.
2. Ask, "If my best friend, mentor, or someone who loves me were here, what would they say to me right now?"
3. Say those words to yourself, out loud if possible.

Why It Works

It creates distance between you and your negative thoughts. Your inner critic operates automatically, but this practice interrupts it by introducing a compassionate perspective.

The "Self-Compassion Post-it Challenge"

Your environment influences your thoughts more than you realize. The goal of this challenge is to surround yourself with self-compassion reminders so that kindness becomes part of your daily routine.

Instructions

1. Write down self-compassionate statements on small sticky notes. Examples:
    - "You are enough just as you are."
    - "It's okay to have bad days."
    - "Perfection is not required."
2. Place them where you'll see them frequently:
    - on your mirror
    - inside your planner
    - on your computer screen
3. Commit to reading at least one aloud each day.

Why It Works

Repetition is key to rewiring your brain (Naz, 2024). Seeing these messages regularly helps counteract negative self-talk and build self-kindness.

"Reparenting" Your Inner Child

A big part of self-compassion is healing the wounds of your past. Many of your self-judgments come from childhood experiences, times when you felt unheard, unloved, or pressured to be perfect. Reparenting is the act of giving yourself the love and reassurance you might not have received.

Instructions

1. Close your eyes and picture yourself as a child.
2. Imagine yourself as the loving, compassionate adult you wish you had.
3. Speak to your inner child:
    - *I see you. I love you. You are safe with me.*
    - *You don't have to be perfect to be loved.*
    - *I am here to take care of you now.*
4. Whenever self-doubt creeps in, remind yourself that you are now in charge of treating yourself with kindness.

Why It Works

Your brain doesn't distinguish between past and present emotions (Gibson, 2024). When you comfort your inner child, you heal deep-rooted wounds and teach yourself that you are worthy of love.

The "Mental Hug" Technique

Physical affection is known to trigger positive emotions, but what if you're alone or don't have someone to comfort you? A mental hug is a self-soothing technique that can replicate the warmth of human connection.

Instructions

1. Close your eyes and take a deep breath.
2. Visualize someone who deeply cares for you giving you a warm, reassuring hug.
3. Feel the sensation of comfort, safety, and love in your body.
4. If possible, hug yourself physically by wrapping your arms around your body.

Why It Works

The brain doesn't always differentiate between real and imagined experiences (Gibson, 2024). Simply imagining warmth and kindness can produce the same calming effects as receiving an actual hug.

Self-Compassion Walks

Sometimes, kindness toward yourself requires stepping away from your usual environment and moving your body. A self-compassion walk combines movement with positive self-talk.

Instructions

1. Take a walk alone, preferably in nature.
2. As you walk, practice self-compassionate thoughts:
    - *I am doing my best, and that is enough.*
    - *I deserve kindness and rest.*
    - *I don't have to be perfect to be worthy.*
3. With each step, imagine leaving behind self-criticism and carrying self-acceptance forward.

Why It Works

Movement releases endorphins, which naturally boost your mood (Perera, 2024). Pairing it with self-compassion reinforces positive sentiments.

The "Permission to Be Human" List

Many people hold themselves to impossible standards, expecting constant productivity, perfection, or stability. This practice helps you embrace your imperfections by acknowledging your humanity.

Instructions

1. Take a piece of paper and title it **"Permission to Be Human."**
2. Write down all the things you tend to judge yourself for.
    - "It's okay if I feel tired and unmotivated sometimes."
    - "It's okay if I don't have all the answers right now."
    - "It's okay if I need help and support from others."
3. Read this list whenever self-criticism arises. You can also add new items over time.

Why It Works

It reframes self-judgment as a natural part of being human. Instead of seeing your struggles as personal failures, you learn to accept them with compassion.

The "Self-Compassion Alarm"

Most people set alarms to wake up or remind them of tasks. But what if your alarms reminded you to be kind to yourself?

Instructions

1. Set a daily alarm on your phone with a self-compassionate message as the label.
    - "You are doing your best, and that's enough."
    - "Pause. Breathe. Be kind to yourself."
    - "You deserve love, even on hard days."
2. When the alarm goes off, take a deep breath and let the message sink in.

Why It Works

This interrupts automatic negative thinking and reminds you to practice self-kindness throughout the day (Neff, 2009).

The No-Pressure Hobby

Many people tie their worth to productivity. A "no-pressure hobby" is an activity you do just for the joy of it, with no goals, no expectations.

Instructions

1. Choose a hobby that interests you (painting, playing music, gardening, or doing puzzles).
2. Set one rule: This is just for fun. No judgment allowed.
3. Whenever self-criticism creeps in, remind yourself: *I don't have to be good at this to enjoy it.*

Why It Works:

It teaches you to experience joy without conditions, which strengthens your ability to be kind to yourself in other areas of life.

The Compassion Stone

This is a tangible way to remind yourself of self-compassion throughout the day.

Instructions

1. Find a small, smooth stone or object that fits in your pocket.
2. Every morning, hold it and set an intention:
   - "This stone reminds me to be gentle with myself today."
3. Throughout the day, whenever you feel self-doubt, touch the stone and repeat a self-compassionate thought.

Why It Works

Physical objects create strong mental associations (Kwok et al., 2018). The act of touching the stone grounds you in the present and brings kindness back to your awareness.

Adopting self-compassion allows you to silence the harsh inner critic and move forward with a greater sense of acceptance. But even with a kinder mindset, stress can still creep in, triggering old negative thought patterns. Learning how to calm both your mind and body is essential to maintaining progress. The upcoming chapter explores powerful relaxation techniques, such as deep breathing and visualization, that can help you manage stress effectively and prevent negativity from taking root.

7

UTILIZING RELAXATION TECHNIQUES

Did you know that deep breathing can literally change your brain?

Studies show that practicing slow, controlled breaths can shrink the amygdala, the part of your brain responsible for fear and stress, making you less reactive to negative thoughts (Balban et al., 2023).

Right now, your mind might feel like a web of overthinking, tangled with doubt and anxiety. Maybe you catch yourself constantly analyzing past interactions, wondering if you said the wrong thing, or worrying about how others perceived you. Perhaps you struggle to move forward because you're fixated on choices you didn't make, fearing you missed the "perfect" path. When your brain is running at full speed, slowing down might feel unproductive if you should be using that energy to solve problems or plan ahead. But the truth is, just like a muscle that's been overworked, your mind needs moments of stillness to function at its best.

Relaxation isn't about ignoring problems or pretending stress doesn't exist. It's about creating space between *you* and your thoughts, giving you the clarity to respond rather than react. Whether it's progressive muscle relaxation easing tension from your shoulders, guided imagery transporting you to a peaceful setting, or mindfulness anchoring you in the present moment, these techniques allow you to hit the mental reset button.

By learning how to truly relax, you'll break free from the grip of self-doubt and cultivate an inner calm that helps you navigate challenges with confidence.

So, let's learn some relaxation tools that will empower you to quiet your mind, recharge your energy, and take control of your thoughts, one deep breath at a time.

HOW RELAXATION TECHNIQUES REDUCE STRESS AND NEGATIVE THINKING

Think of your brain like a phone that's constantly running dozens of apps in the background. Every worry, doubt, or overanalyzed conversation is an app draining your mental battery. If you never close these mental tabs, your mind becomes overloaded, sluggish, and prone to errors, just like a phone starts lagging. That's where relaxation techniques come in. They work like a force quit, shutting down unnecessary stress responses and freeing up mental space for clarity and rational thinking.

The Science Behind Stress and Relaxation

When you're stressed, your brain triggers the fight-or-flight response, flooding your system with cortisol and adrenaline. These stress hormones are great for handling immediate danger, like jumping out of the way of a speeding car (Tindle & Tadi, 2022).. However, when they're constantly activated by daily stressors and self-doubt, they do more harm than good. Chronic stress can lead to increased heart rate, muscle tension, trouble sleeping, and, most importantly, negative thought patterns that make you doubt yourself.

Relaxation techniques, on the other hand, activate the PNS, which is responsible for the "rest and digest" state. This helps lower your heart rate, reduce muscle tension, and above all, calm the whirlwind of thoughts that fuel anxiety and overthinking (Tindle & Tadi, 2022).

By shifting your brain from a reactive state to a relaxed one, you weaken the grip of negative thoughts and create mental space to think clearly and rationally. Instead of automatically believing every self-doubting thought that pops into your head, you can observe it, question it, and decide whether it actually deserves your attention.

EFFECTIVE RELAXATION TECHNIQUES

Now that you understand how relaxation techniques help rewire your brain for calmness and clarity, the next step is learning how to put them into action. True relaxation helps you feel good in the moment. It also trains your mind to respond differently to stress, anxiety, and self-doubt. The more consistently you practice, the stronger your mental resilience becomes.

We have already covered some techniques in Chapter 4. Now, we will discuss some other highly effective relaxation techniques that will help you shift from self-doubt to self-assurance.

Autogenic Training: Rewiring Your Mind for Relaxation

Autogenic training (AT) is a relaxation technique that uses self-suggestion to bring on a deep state of relaxation. Developed by German psychiatrist Johannes Schultz, AT works by focusing on physical sensations (warmth, heaviness, and calmness) to reduce stress and self-doubt. It's a great tool for anyone who struggles with overthinking and needs a structured way to regain control of their thoughts (Breznoscakova et al., 2023).

Instructions

1. Sit or lie down in a quiet place where you won't be disturbed.
2. Close your eyes and take a few deep breaths.
3. Repeat the following phrases in your mind, slowly and intentionally:

- "My arms and legs feel heavy and warm."
- "My heartbeat is calm and steady."
- "My breathing is slow and regular."
- "I feel completely relaxed and at peace."
4. Visualize warmth spreading through your body, starting from your feet and moving upward.
5. Continue for 10–15 minutes, allowing your body to fully embrace the sensation of relaxation.

Why It Works

AT uses self-suggestion to shift your nervous system into relaxation mode. By focusing on warm, heavy sensations, you create a sense of deep physical and mental calm (Breznoscakova et al., 2023). Over time, this technique helps reduce self-doubt by reinforcing a sense of control over your body and mind.

Tactile Grounding: Using Touch to Interrupt Negative Thoughts

When negative thoughts go out of control, your mind feels disconnected from reality. Grounding techniques help bring you back to the present moment by engaging your senses. Tactile grounding, in particular, uses physical touch to redirect your focus and calm your nerves.

Instructions

1. Find an object with an interesting texture, like a smooth stone, a soft blanket, or a beaded bracelet.
2. Hold it in your hands and focus on its texture, temperature, and weight.
3. Run your fingers over it slowly, paying attention to every detail.
4. If your mind starts drifting into negative thoughts, bring your attention back to the sensation of touch.

Why It Works

Your brain can't focus on two things at once (Weaver, 2024). By concentrating on a physical sensation, you shift your attention away from anxious or self-doubting thoughts. This technique is especially useful during moments of high stress, as it provides an immediate way to regain control.

HAVENING: REWIRING YOUR EMOTIONAL RESPONSES

Havening is a self-soothing technique that involves stroking your arms, face, or hands in a rhythmic motion to trigger a relaxation response (Villines, 2023). It's particularly effective for reducing emotional overwhelm and quieting self-doubt.

Instructions

1. Cross your arms over your chest and slowly stroke from your shoulders down to your elbows.
2. Repeat this gentle motion while thinking of a calming word or phrase, such as *I am safe* or *I am enough*.
3. Continue for a few minutes, focusing on the soothing sensation.

Why It Works

Havening stimulates delta waves in the brain, which are associated with deep relaxation and emotional regulation (Villines, 2023). This practice provides immediate relief from stress and helps reframe negative thoughts into more empowering ones.

Laughter Therapy: The Science of Laughing Away Stress

Laughter is one of the fastest ways to reduce stress hormones and boost your mood. Even if you don't feel like laughing, forcing yourself to smile or laugh can still trigger the brain to release feel-good chemicals like endorphins (Yim, 2016).

Instructions

1. Watch a funny video, listen to a comedy podcast, or recall a hilarious memory.
2. If you're alone, try laughing intentionally. Yes, even fake laughter works!
3. Notice how your mood shifts within minutes.

Why It Works

Laughter reduces cortisol levels and increases serotonin, which helps counteract negative thought patterns. It also gives a mental break from overthinking, allowing you to regain perspective and lighten up (Yim, 2016).

Shaking Therapy: Releasing Stress Through Movement

Animals shake off stress instinctively; after escaping danger, a dog or deer will often shake their whole body to reset their nervous system. Humans, however, tend to hold onto stress physically. Shaking therapy mimics this natural response to release built-up tension (Vinall, 2021).

Instructions

1. Stand up and shake your arms, legs, and head lightly.
2. Gradually increase the intensity, shaking your entire body for one to two minutes.
3. Slow down and take a few deep breaths, noticing the difference in how you feel.

Why It Works

Shaking stimulates the nervous system, releasing stored stress and breaking the cycle of tension (Vinall, 2021). It's especially helpful if you feel physically restless or emotionally stuck.

Acupressure: Pressing Away Anxiety

Acupressure is based on the same principles as acupuncture but uses gentle pressure instead of needles (Raypole, 2024). By stimulating certain points in the body, you can reduce stress and restore balance to your nervous system.

Instructions

1. Locate the *Hegu* (LI4) point, found between the thumb and index finger.
2. Apply firm pressure and massage in small circles for 30 seconds.
3. Breathe deeply and focus on the sensation.

Why It Works

Acupressure releases tension and increases circulation, which helps lower stress and anxiety (Raypole, 2024). It's a quick, discreet way to calm yourself in moments of self-doubt.

Progressive Muscle Relaxation (PMR): Releasing Tension, Releasing Doubt

Your body and mind are deeply connected. When your muscles are tense, your thoughts tend to be rigid and anxious. PMR is a method that helps release physical tension in a systematic way, sending signals to your brain that it's safe to relax (Toussaint et al., 2021). This technique is especially useful if you struggle with chronic stress, overthinking, or self-doubt that manifests as physical tightness in your body.

Instructions

1. Find a quiet place and sit or lie down comfortably.
2. Close your eyes and take a few deep breaths.
3. Start with your feet: Squeeze the muscles in your toes and feet as tightly as you can for five seconds, then release.

4. Move upward through your body, tensing and relaxing each muscle group—calves, thighs, stomach, chest, arms, shoulders, neck, and face.
5. Pay attention to the difference between tension and relaxation as you move through each area.
6. After completing the full body, take a deep breath and enjoy the sensation of lightness.

Why It Works

PMR helps reset your nervous system by reducing overall muscle tension and increasing bodily awareness (Toussaint et al., 2021). The process also encourages mindfulness, helping you become more present rather than getting lost in anxious thoughts. By actively relaxing your muscles, you send a powerful message to your brain: "You are in control. You are safe. You are capable."

Floating Meditation: The Weightlessness Effect

If you've ever floated in the water, you know the deeply calming effect it has on your body. Floating meditation mimics this sensation, either through sensory deprivation in a float tank or simply lying on a soft surface and imagining the feeling of weightlessness. This technique is particularly helpful for those who feel overwhelmed by their thoughts and need a way to detach from stress (*What Is a Floating Meditation Tank?*, 2024)..

Instructions

1. Lie down on a comfortable surface, preferably on your back.
2. Close your eyes and imagine that your body is floating in water.
3. Release all tension and let your limbs become heavy.
4. Focus on your breath, allowing yourself to "drift" deeper into relaxation.
5. Stay in this state for 10–15 minutes, enjoying the sensation of floating.

Why It Works

Floating meditation helps quiet the mind by reducing sensory input. It encourages deep relaxation, lowers stress hormones, and creates a sense of mental and physical lightness (*What Is a Floating Meditation Tank?*, 2024). By "letting go," you practice surrendering control over negative thoughts and replacing them with inner peace.

Self-Massage: Easing Stress Through Touch

Massage isn't just for luxury spas. It's a proven method for reducing muscle tension and promoting relaxation (Weerapong et al., 2005). Even a simple self-massage can lower stress and help you feel more grounded.

Instructions

1. Use your fingers to massage your temples gently in circular motions.
2. Press into the tension points in your shoulders and neck, kneading gently.
3. Roll a tennis ball under your feet or along your back against a wall for a deeper massage.

Why It Works

Massage stimulates circulation and reduces muscle tightness, sending calming signals to your brain (Weerapong et al., 2005). It also helps shift your focus away from stress and into the physical sensations of relaxation.

Nature Therapy: The Healing Power of Green Spaces

Spending time in nature, whether in a park, garden, or by a body of water, has a healthy effect on mental well-being.

Instructions

1. Step outside and take a short walk in a green space.
2. Focus on natural elements around you—listen to birds, feel the breeze, notice the colors.
3. If you can't go outside, look at pictures of nature or listen to nature sounds.

Why It Works

Nature provides a sense of calm and perspective, helping you disconnect from stressful thoughts and reconnect with the present. Studies show that being in natural environments reduces cortisol levels and enhances mood (Jimenez, 2021).

Journaling for Emotional Release

Writing down your thoughts allows you to process emotions, gain clarity, and let go of stress. Journaling helps shift your focus from dwelling on problems to finding solutions.

Instructions

1. Set a timer for 5–10 minutes.
2. Write down whatever is on your mind—without filtering or judging.
3. If you're stuck, try prompts like:
    - "What's worrying me right now?"
    - "What can I control in this situation?"
    - "What am I grateful for today?"

Why It Works

Journaling gives your thoughts a safe space to exist outside of your mind, reducing mental clutter and providing emotional relief.

Slow Stretching: Unwinding the Mind Through Movement

Stress often makes your body tighten up, leading to stiffness and discomfort. Gentle stretching helps release tension and promotes a sense of ease.

Instructions

1. Roll your shoulders back and forth.
2. Slowly tilt your head side to side, releasing neck tension.
3. Stretch your arms overhead and take a deep breath.
4. Hold each stretch for at least 20 seconds, breathing deeply.

Why It Works

Stretching improves circulation, reduces muscle tightness, and helps shift your nervous system into a more relaxed state (Imagawa et al., 2023).

Coloring and Creative Play

Engaging in simple, creative activities like coloring, doodling, or crafting induces a state of relaxation similar to meditation.

Instructions

1. Grab a coloring book, sketchpad, or craft supplies.
2. Focus on the process rather than the result.
3. Let your mind wander as you create without judgment.

Why It Works

Creative activities engage the brain in a way that lowers stress and promotes mindfulness, allowing you to unwind naturally (Martin et al., 2018).

Singing for Stress Relief: The Power of Vocal Expression

Singing is a natural form of emotional release that helps regulate breathing, eases tension, and boosts confidence (Jäncke, 2008).

Instructions

1. Pick a song that lifts your mood.
2. Sing out loud, focusing on the rhythm and melody.
3. Don't worry about how you sound—let yourself enjoy the moment.
4. If you prefer, hum instead of singing.

Why It Works

Singing engages the diaphragm, promoting deep breathing and relaxation. It also releases feel-good chemicals in the brain, reducing stress (Jäncke, 2008).

Cloud Watching: A Mindful Escape

Looking up at the sky and watching clouds float by is a simple yet powerful way to calm the mind. It shifts your focus from stress to the vastness of nature.

Instructions

1. Lie down outside or sit by a window with a view of the sky.
2. Observe the movement and shapes of the clouds.
3. Take slow breaths, syncing your breathing with the clouds' movement.
4. Let your thoughts drift like clouds, allowing them to pass without judgment.

Why It Works

Cloud watching induces mindfulness, creating a sense of peace and perspective. It also helps disengage from overthinking and promotes relaxation.

Scent Therapy: Using Aromas to Shift Your Mood

Certain scents have a direct impact on brain chemistry, helping to reduce anxiety, improve focus, or promote deep relaxation (Walsh, 2020).

Instructions

1. Choose a calming scent, such as lavender, chamomile, or sandalwood.
2. Inhale deeply from an essential oil bottle, diffuser, or scented candle.
3. Focus on the aroma and how it makes you feel.
4. Use scent as part of your relaxation routine, associating it with calmness.

Why It Works

The olfactory system is directly linked to the brain's emotional center, meaning scents can quickly shift your mood and relax your body (Walsh, 2020).

Watching Fish or Water Movements

The smooth, repetitive motion of water or fish creates a calming effect on the brain, reducing mental noise.

Instructions

1. If you have an aquarium, spend time watching the fish move.
2. If not, find a video of flowing water or an aquarium livestream.
3. Breathe slowly as you observe the movement.

Why It Works

Watching fish swim or water ripple has been shown to lower stress and induce a meditative state (*Aquatic Therapy*, 2024).

Slow Eating: Mindful Bites for Relaxation

Slowing down your eating pace encourages mindfulness and relaxation.

Instructions

1. Take a small bite of food.
2. Chew slowly, noticing the texture and taste.
3. Put your utensils down between bites.

Why It Works

Mindful eating engages the senses and helps shift your focus from stress to the present moment.

Candle Meditation: Focusing the Mind Through Flame

Candle meditation, also known as Trataka, is a simple yet powerful technique that involves gazing at a flickering flame to quiet the mind and enhance focus (Mayer, 2022). This practice is often used in yoga and mindfulness traditions to improve concentration and create a deep state of relaxation.

Instructions

1. Find a quiet, dimly lit room and place a candle at eye level, about two to three feet away from you. Ensure you are sitting comfortably with your spine straight.
2. Light the candle and softly focus on the flame without blinking too much. Allow your vision to settle on the movement of the flame.
3. Inhale slowly through your nose, hold for a moment, and then exhale fully. Maintain this steady breathing rhythm as you continue gazing.
4. If thoughts arise, acknowledge them and gently return your focus to the flame.
5. After 5-10 minutes, close your eyes and visualize the flame in

your mind's eye. Stay in this meditative state for a few more minutes before opening your eyes.

Why It Works

The rhythmic flickering of the flame engages your mind, acting as an anchor that prevents overthinking (Mayer, 2022). This practice enhances mindfulness, reduces stress, and improves mental clarity.

Relaxation techniques help regulate your nervous system, making it easier to respond to challenges with clarity rather than anxiety. But no one thrives in isolation; your environment and relationships also influence your mental state. Support from others can provide encouragement, validation, and a fresh perspective when you need it most. In the next chapter, you'll discover how to build a strong support system, seek out positive connections, and harness the power of community to reinforce a healthier mindset.

8

SEEKING SOCIAL SUPPORT

You sit in your car, staring at your phone, debating whether to call a friend. It's been a rough week: work stress, self-doubt, and that all-too-familiar voice in your head whispering, *No one really wants to hear about your problems.* You almost convince yourself to go home and deal with it alone, just like always. But then, you remember Mary.

Mary used to do the same thing, bottle everything up, convinced that asking for help was a burden. She prided herself on being independent, the "strong one" in her friend group. But when she hit rock bottom, struggling with overwhelming anxiety, she finally reached out to a close friend. To her surprise, that one conversation didn't just lighten her load. It strengthened their friendship. Over time, she built a support system that helped her silence the self-doubt and navigate life's challenges with more confidence.

Like Mary, you might believe you have to figure everything out on your own. But emotional resilience isn't about handling everything alone; it's about knowing when to lean on others. The right kind of support can change the way you see yourself, your problems, and your ability to overcome them.

IMPORTANCE OF CONNECTING WITH OTHERS

When you're stuck in a cycle of self-doubt and overthinking, isolation can be your worst enemy. Your mind can become a chamber, amplifying negative thoughts without any outside perspective to challenge them. Social connections can play a crucial role in regulating emotions. When you talk to someone who understands you, it activates the brain's reward system, releasing oxytocin and reducing stress hormones like cortisol.

Think about the last time you vented to a close friend. Maybe you walked away from the conversation feeling a little lighter, a little less alone. That's not just emotional relief. In fact, it's a biological response. Humans are wired for connection. Without it, negative thoughts have room to spiral unchecked, making problems seem bigger than they are.

The Myth of Self-Sufficiency

You might believe that handling everything on your own is a sign of strength. After all, society often glorifies self-reliance, painting the image of the lone wolf who figures things out without help. When you can't do it in real life, you start to question your abilities. What you miss while judging yourself harshly is that you are trying to do something that is unrealistic. You can do something on your own, but you can't do everything on your own. You will need to ask for help, and that is more than okay.

But the real strength lies in knowing when to reach out. Some of the most successful and emotionally intelligent people actively seek support from friends, mentors, or support groups.

Take the example of Michael Phelps, one of the most celebrated Olympians in history (Cassata, 2022). At the height of his career, he struggled with depression and considered ending his life. It wasn't until he opened up to friends and sought professional help that he was able to regain control. Even someone as accomplished as Phelps needed support, proving that no amount of success makes you immune to self-doubt.

How the Right People Can Shift Your Mindset

The people you surround yourself with influence your thoughts more than you realize. If you regularly engage with supportive, positive people, their perspectives help reframe your self-doubt. On the other hand, if you confide in people who dismiss your feelings or reinforce negativity, your inner critic only grows stronger.

Imagine you're struggling with a difficult decision at work. You confide in one friend who says, "You always overthink things. Just stop worrying." That response might make you feel invalidated, even ashamed. But another friend listens, acknowledges your feelings, and says, "I get why this is tough. What's the worst that could happen? Let's figure it out together."

The second response doesn't just comfort you. It challenges your overthinking. It gives a different, more balanced perspective, making the problem seem more manageable.

The Fear of Reaching Out

Even when you know social support is valuable, actually reaching out can feel terrifying. You may worry about being judged, rejected, or seen as weak. But ask yourself, if a friend came to you struggling with self-doubt, would you see them as weak? Or would you feel honored that they trusted you enough to open up?

Most people are more willing to listen than we assume. In fact, research suggests that people tend to feel closer to those who confide in them (DePaulo, 2014). Vulnerability strengthens relationships, creating deeper and more meaningful connections.

So the next time you hesitate to reach out, remind yourself that asking for support isn't a burden. Instead, it's an opportunity to build stronger relationships and break free from the cycle of negative thinking.

How Sharing Your Experience Brings Clarity

When you're lost in your own thoughts, problems can feel enormous and unsolvable. But something shifts when you put those thoughts into words. Speaking them aloud forces your brain to organize them, making them feel less overwhelming. Even before someone responds, just hearing yourself explain a problem can make it feel more manageable.

Think about the last time you gave advice to a friend who was struggling. It was probably easier to see solutions for them than it is when you're stuck in your own head, right? That's because problems often feel bigger when they're yours. When you talk things through with someone else, they offer a fresh perspective that you might not have considered.

The Power of Perspective-Shifting Conversations

Sometimes, the real issue isn't the situation itself. It's the way you're looking at it. When self-skepticism takes over, you might catastrophize, assuming the worst will happen. But the right conversation with the right person can shift your entire perspective.

That moment of reassurance doesn't erase the mistake, but it reframes it. Instead of seeing yourself as a failure, you start to realize that one mistake doesn't define you. The same situation that felt like the end of the world just minutes ago now seems like a small bump in the road.

Finding Relief Through Shared Experiences

Have you ever opened up to someone about a struggle, only to hear them say, "I know exactly how that feels"? That moment of connection can be incredibly wonderful. It reminds you that you're not alone and that your struggles aren't unique or insurmountable.

This is why support groups and online communities exist. Whether it's anxiety, imposter syndrome, or career struggles, people often find relief in knowing that others have faced the same challenges and made it through. Even informal conversations with friends or colleagues can have the same effect.

Take Brené Brown, for example, a researcher known for her work on vulnerability and shame (*Brené Brown on Shame and Accountability*, 2020). She emphasizes that shame thrives in silence but loses its power when spoken aloud. The more you share, the less isolated you feel, and the easier it becomes to break free from negative thought patterns.

When You Can't See a Way Forward, Others Can

Sometimes, self-doubt clouds your judgment so much that you can't see solutions right in front of you. This is where trusted friends, mentors, or even therapists come in. They offer a clearer view, not because they're smarter or stronger, but because they aren't weighed down by your internal doubts.

Picture this: You've been considering applying for a promotion but keep convincing yourself that you're not qualified. You tell a friend about your hesitations, expecting them to agree. Instead, they remind you of all the times you successfully handled difficult projects and how much you've grown in your role. Suddenly, the story you've been telling yourself (that you're not good enough) doesn't hold up.

That's the power of external support. It challenges your self-doubt and offers a more balanced, realistic view of your abilities.

The Fear of Judgment vs. The Reality of Support

The fear of being judged can keep you from opening up, but in reality, people are often more understanding than you expect. Vulnerability tends to draw people closer, not push them away.

Think about the moments when someone has confided in you. Did you judge them? Or did you feel honored that they trusted you enough to share? Most of the time, we respond to vulnerability with empathy, yet we assume others will judge us when we're the ones opening up.

By breaking through that fear and allowing yourself to seek support, you not only gain relief but also strengthen your relationships in ways you never expected.

The Science Behind Talking It Out

There's a reason why sharing your thoughts can bring relief. Research suggests that verbalizing emotions helps reduce their intensity. When you put your feelings into words, you activate the brain's prefrontal cortex, the area responsible for rational thinking, while calming down the amygdala, which is responsible for fear and emotional reactions (Conway, 2021).

This means that simply talking about what's bothering you can help you process emotions more clearly. It's why people often say they feel "lighter" after venting to a friend. It's not just emotional support; it's a neurological shift that helps quiet your overactive thoughts.

EXERCISES TO BUILD SOCIAL CONNECTIONS

Taking small steps toward connection might feel uncomfortable at first, but like any skill, the more you practice, the easier it becomes. You don't have to force yourself into overwhelming social situations. Instead, focus on simple, intentional exercises that help you gradually build confidence in your ability to connect with others. These exercises are designed to strengthen your social skills, ease self-doubt, and create meaningful relationships.

The "One Compliment a Day" Challenge

Giving compliments is a simple yet healthy way to initiate social interactions and strengthen relationships. It shifts your focus from self-doubt to appreciation for others, making it easier to engage in positive conversations.

Instructions

1. Each day, give one genuine compliment to someone. It could be a friend, a colleague, or even a stranger.
2. Keep it simple but sincere:
    - "I love how organized you are—it's really inspiring!"
    - "That color looks amazing on you!"

- "You have such a great sense of humor. You always make people laugh!"
3. Observe their reaction. Most people appreciate compliments and respond warmly, creating an easy opportunity for connection.

Why It Works

This exercise shifts your mindset from self-consciousness to outward appreciation. When you focus on making others feel good, social interactions become less intimidating. It also reinforces the idea that positive interactions don't have to be complicated. They can start with something as simple as kind words.

The "30-Second Courage" Rule

Many opportunities for connection are lost because of hesitation. This exercise helps you override self-doubt by committing to brief moments of courage.

Instructions

1. When you feel nervous about speaking up, be it starting a conversation, joining a discussion, or sending a message, count down from 3 and take action within 30 seconds.
2. Examples of when to apply this rule:
    - sending a message to an old friend
    - saying hello to a coworker
    - introducing yourself to someone at an event
3. The key is not giving your brain time to overthink or talk you out of it.

Why It Works

Self-doubt thrives in hesitation. By taking action quickly, you interrupt negative thought loops and prove to yourself that social interactions aren't as scary as they seem.

The "Shared Experience" Invitation

Stronger connections are often built through shared experiences rather than surface-level conversations. This exercise helps you create opportunities for deeper bonds.

Instructions

1. Think of an activity you enjoy or want to try: hiking, a movie night, a coffee meetup, or an online game.
2. Invite someone to join you, framing it as a casual opportunity to share the experience together. For example:
   - "Hey, I'm planning to check out this new café. Want to come along?"
   - "I'm thinking of watching [movie title] this weekend. Want to join?"
3. Keep the invitation low-pressure, making it easy for the other person to say yes.

Why It Works

People often hesitate to make plans because they assume others are too busy or uninterested. By initiating shared experiences, you create natural opportunities for connection while reducing the pressure of forced conversation.

The "Social Mindfulness" Practice

Social interactions feel more fulfilling when you're fully present. This exercise trains you to be more engaged in conversations, helping you build deeper connections.

Instructions

1. The next time you're in a conversation, focus on active listening:
   - maintain eye contact
   - nod or give small verbal affirmations ("That makes sense," "I see what you mean")

- resist the urge to plan your response while the other person is speaking
2. After the conversation, reflect on one thing the person shared and follow up later ("You mentioned you had a big meeting—how did it go?").

Why It Works

When people feel truly heard, they feel valued. Practicing mindfulness in conversations makes interactions more meaningful and helps you become a better communicator.

The "Join & Engage" Experiment

Meeting new people can feel daunting, but engaging in shared activities makes it easier. This exercise encourages gradual social expansion in a structured way.

Instructions

1. Choose a group or activity that interests you: a fitness class, book club, online forum, or professional networking event.
2. Attend at least one session with the goal of speaking to at least one person.
3. If starting conversations feels difficult, ask simple, open-ended questions:
    - "How long have you been coming here?"
    - "What got you interested in this?"

Why It Works

Joining a group provides built-in social opportunities without the pressure of one-on-one interactions. Over time, you'll become more comfortable engaging with new people.

The "One Positive Social Interaction" Tracker

When you struggle with suspicion, it's easy to overlook positive social experiences. This exercise helps you recognize and reinforce successful interactions.

Instructions

1. Each day, write down one positive social interaction, big or small. For example:
    - "Had a great chat with my coworker at lunch."
    - "A friend texted to check in on me."
    - "A stranger held the door open and smiled."
2. Review your list at the end of each week to remind yourself that social connection is happening more often than you think.

Why It Works

Tracking positive experiences shifts your focus from what's missing to what's already going well, building confidence in your social abilities.

The "Five-Minute Favor" Strategy

Offering help to others, even in small ways, strengthens social bonds and makes you feel more connected. This exercise encourages acts of kindness that take no more than five minutes but have lasting effects.

Instructions

1. Identify small ways you can help someone, such as:
    - offering to proofread a friend's resume.
    - bringing coffee for a colleague.
    - sharing a useful resource or article.
2. Aim to complete one five-minute favor per week.

Why It Works

Acts of kindness trigger positive social responses, making it easier to build and maintain relationships. Giving support also strengthens the idea that social connection is a two-way street.

The "Open-Ended Question" Habit

Conversations often die out quickly because they rely on yes/no answers. This exercise helps you create deeper discussions and build rapport by using open-ended questions.

Instructions

1. In your next conversation, replace yes/no questions with open-ended ones:
    - Instead of "Did you have a good weekend?" ask, "What was the highlight of your weekend?"
    - Instead of "Do you like your job?" ask, "What's your favorite part about what you do?"
2. Notice how the conversation flows more naturally and feels more engaging.

Why It Works

Open-ended questions encourage more meaningful dialogue, making interactions feel richer and more fulfilling. They also show genuine interest in others, strengthening connections.

The "Social Wins" Journal

Self-doubt can make you believe that you struggle socially, even when you have successful interactions. This exercise helps you recognize your progress by tracking small social wins.

Instructions

1. Keep a journal where you write down small social successes. You can start with promotes such as:
    - "I started a conversation with someone new."

- "I reconnected with an old friend."
- "I spoke up in a group discussion."
2. Read back through your entries weekly to see how far you've come.

Why It Works

This exercise retrains your mindset to acknowledge and celebrate social progress, boosting confidence.

The "Social Media Engagement" Shift

Many people passively scroll through social media without engaging, strengthening feelings of isolation. This exercise encourages active participation to foster connection.

Instructions

1. Each day, comment on one post instead of just liking it.
2. Send a supportive message to someone you haven't talked to in a while.
3. Share something positive and invite discussion (for example, "What's the best book you've read lately?").

Why It Works

Social media can be a tool for connection rather than comparison. Actively engaging in conversations online strengthens relationships and creates more opportunities for real-world connections.

Surrounding yourself with supportive people reminds you that you're not alone in your struggles. But even with external encouragement, having a clear sense of direction is crucial to staying motivated and positive. Without meaningful goals, it's easy to fall back into old habits of self-doubt and hesitation. The upcoming chapter focuses on setting realistic and achievable goals that create a sense of purpose, build confidence, and reinforce the progress you've made.

9

SETTING REALISTIC GOALS

Imagine yourself standing at the base of a mountain, eager to reach the peak. You're filled with ambition, but without a clear path, the climb feels overwhelming. This is what goal-setting often feels like: an exciting yet difficult task. You have dreams, but a lack of certainty tells you that you're aiming too high or that failure is inevitable. The truth is, success isn't about chasing unrealistic ideals or making leaps beyond your reach; it's about taking steady, intentional steps in the right direction.

When you break down a massive objective into smaller, tangible steps, progress feels natural rather than exhausting. Think of it as training for a marathon. You wouldn't start by running 26 miles on day one. Instead, you'd build endurance gradually, celebrating each milestone along the way.

Know that your mindset matters just as much as the plan itself. If negative thought patterns are holding you back, even the most well-structured plan will feel out of reach. That's why mastering how to set realistic pursuits means shifting the way you see progress, success, and, most importantly, yourself.

In this chapter, you will learn how to set realistic dreams effectively.

THE ROLE OF GOAL-SETTING IN FOSTERING A POSITIVE MINDSET

The way you approach dreams directly influences how you perceive yourself, your abilities, and your potential for success. When done right, goal-setting isn't just a roadmap; it's a powerful catalyst for breaking free from self-doubt and negative thought patterns.

Every time you create a plan, you're making a statement about what you believe is possible. If your objectives are unrealistic or vague, you might unintentionally reinforce feelings of inadequacy. On the other hand, when you set realistic, well-defined objectives, you create a sense of direction, reinforcing the belief that progress is within your grasp. Each small victory along the way acts as a confidence booster, proving to yourself that you are capable, resourceful, and resilient.

The Psychology Behind Goal-Setting and Positivity

Your brain loves to count on achievement. Accomplishing a plan (no matter how small) activates a release of dopamine, a neurotransmitter linked to motivation and happiness (Martin et al., 2010). This is why checking something off your to-do list feels so satisfying. It's less about the task itself and more about strengthening the belief that you are in control of your progress.

Now, imagine the opposite. If you frequently set plans that are too ambitious without breaking them down into smaller steps, you might end up feeling frustrated rather than motivated. The gap between where you are and where you want to be seems insurmountable, fueling self-doubt instead of confidence. The key is to leverage goal-setting as a tool for fostering a growth-oriented mindset. It should celebrate progress, value persistence, and recognize that success is built through consistency, not overnight transformations.

The Link Between Goal-Setting and Self-Identity

Your ideals shape the way you see yourself. When you set and achieve dreams, you form an identity of competence and perseverance. On the flip side, repeatedly falling short of unrealistic objectives can make you feel like someone who "never follows through" or "just isn't good enough." The way to break this cycle is by aligning your dreams with your evolving identity.

For instance, if you want to develop a habit of reading more, instead of setting a rigid plan like "read 50 books this year," shift your focus to identifying as someone who values reading. A goal like "read for 15 minutes every evening" allows you to build that identity gradually. Over time, as reading becomes a natural part of your routine, finishing books will become a byproduct of this identity shift rather than a forced obligation.

Adopting a Flexible Mindset

One of the biggest mistakes people make when setting objectives is treating them as rigid, unchangeable benchmarks. Life is unpredictable, and sometimes, circumstances shift in ways that require you to adjust your plans. Instead of seeing this as a failure, embrace flexibility as part of the process.

This flexibility also allows you to recalibrate your plans based on new insights. Maybe you started a goal with one vision in mind but later discovered a different path that excites you more. Being open to these shifts helps you stay engaged and prevents feelings of failure when plans don't go exactly as expected.

The Role of Self-Compassion

Perfectionism and harsh self-criticism are major roadblocks to maintaining a positive mindset. If you're too hard on yourself for not achieving a dream exactly as planned, you risk falling into a cycle of discouragement. Instead, practice self-compassion by acknowledging effort rather than just results.

Let's say you set an objective to wake up at 6 a.m. every day to meditate, but you find yourself hitting snooze more often than not. Instead of berating yourself, shift your perspective: "I'm building a new habit, and change takes time. What adjustments can I make to set myself up for success?" Maybe that means starting with three days a week instead of seven or meditating for five minutes instead of twenty. The key is to support yourself through the process rather than punishing yourself for perceived shortcomings.

At its core, it is less about specific achievements and more about how they change your perception of yourself. Each dream you set and accomplish reinforces a narrative about your capabilities. The more you prove to yourself that you can follow through, the more you dismantle self-doubt and replace it with a belief in your ability to grow, adapt, and succeed.

SMART GOALS

If your objectives feel vague, overwhelming, or unrealistic, they can quickly become a source of frustration rather than motivation. That's where the SMART framework comes in, a structured yet flexible approach designed to help you set plans that are clear, actionable, and within your reach.

SMART goals stand for Specific, Measurable, Achievable, Relevant, and Time-bound. This method transforms abstract ambitions into concrete plans, ensuring that every objective you set is not just a wish but a roadmap toward tangible progress.

By breaking down each component, you'll see how this approach empowers you to shift from passive dreaming to intentional action.

S—Specific: Defining with Clarity

Ambiguity breeds uncertainty. When a plan lacks precision, it becomes difficult to track progress or even know where to begin. A specific objective eliminates confusion by answering key questions:

- What do you want to accomplish?
- Why is this dream important to you?
- What steps will you take to achieve it?

For example, saying, "I want to be healthier" is too vague. What does "healthier" mean to you?

Do you want to exercise more, eat better, improve your mental well-being, or do all of the above?

A more specific plan would be: "I want to improve my cardiovascular health by running three times a week for 30 minutes."

Now, you have a clear action plan rather than an abstract intention.

The power of specificity lies in its ability to give you a structure. When you define your target precisely, you reduce uncertainty and set yourself up for success by knowing exactly what needs to be done.

M—Measurable: Tracking Your Progress

Without a way to measure success, it's difficult to stay motivated. Measurable objectives provide benchmarks that allow you to see how far you've come and adjust your approach if needed. This is where numbers, deadlines, or qualitative assessments come into play.

Think of someone who wants to save money. Saying, "I want to save more," lacks a measurable component. Instead, defining the plan as "I will save $200 per month for the next six months" gives a concrete target. Each month, progress can be tracked, and adjustments can be made if necessary.

Tracking progress not only keeps you accountable but also provides a sense of accomplishment along the way. Seeing tangible results reinforces the belief that you are capable of change and growth. Even if progress is slow, measurable indicators ensure that you recognize every step forward.

A—Achievable: Setting Within Reach

Dreaming big is encouraged, but setting objectives that stretch you too far too soon can lead to frustration and self-doubt. Achievable goals balance ambition with practicality; they push you beyond your comfort zone but remain within your ability to accomplish.

For instance, if you've never run before, creating a plan to complete a marathon in a month might set you up for disappointment. Instead, an achievable objective would be: "I will train for a 5K race over the next two months by running three times a week and gradually increasing my distance." This approach acknowledges where you are now while creating a realistic path forward.

R—Relevant: Aligning with Your Purpose

A plan should hold personal meaning. If it doesn't align with your values, priorities, or long-term vision, it's easy to lose motivation. Relevance ensures that your efforts contribute to something that genuinely matters to you.

Imagine someone setting a plan to learn a new language because their friends are doing it, not because they have a personal desire to. Without genuine interest, commitment fades quickly. Instead, a relevant plan might be: "I want to learn Spanish so I can confidently communicate while traveling through South America next year."

When your plans align with your passions and aspirations, motivation becomes intrinsic. You're not just chasing an arbitrary milestone; you're working toward something that enhances your life in a meaningful way.

T—Time-Bound: Creating a Sense of Urgency

A goal without a deadline can easily be postponed indefinitely. Time-bound objectives establish a clear timeframe, preventing procrastination and keeping you focused.

Saying, "I want to write a book someday," lacks urgency. Instead, refining the plan to "I will write 500 words a day and complete my first draft within six months" sets a clear timeframe for progress. This structure transforms your ambition into a series of actionable steps rather than an open-ended wish.

Deadlines create a sense of accountability, helping you stay on track even when motivation wavers. However, they should be flexible enough to adapt if necessary. Life happens, and unexpected circumstances may require adjustments. The key is to use time constraints as a motivational tool rather than a source of pressure.

The Reverse Engineering Method

Instead of starting with where you are and wondering how to move forward, this practice flips the process. You begin with the end objective and work backward, identifying each step needed to achieve it. This approach prevents overwhelming yourself with a massive dream while helping you visualize a clear path forward.

Instructions

1. Write down a long-term goal you want to achieve (e.g., "I want to launch my own business in a year").
2. Imagine you have already achieved it—picture what that success looks like.
3. Break it down into major milestones. If you want to launch a business, milestones could be:
   - conduct market research
   - develop a business plan
   - secure funding
   - create a product/service prototype
   - launch marketing efforts
4. For each milestone, break it down into smaller, manageable steps with specific timeframes.
5. Once you reach the present moment, identify what the very first step is and take action.

Why It Works

This method makes even the most ambitious dreams feel achievable by giving you a step-by-step roadmap.

The "Why" Ladder

Self-doubt often stems from a lack of clarity about why a dream matters. This practice helps you look deep into your motivation, reinforcing your commitment and helping you set meaningful objectives that align with your values.

Instructions

1. Write down a dream you want to achieve (e.g., "I want to exercise more").
2. Ask yourself: *Why do I want to achieve this?* Write down your answer.
3. Take your answer and ask **why** again.
4. Repeat this process five times, going deeper with each layer.

Example:

- "I want to exercise more."
- **Why?** "Because I want to feel healthier."
- **Why?** "Because I want to have more energy."
- **Why?** "Because I feel sluggish and tired all the time."
- **Why?** "Because I'm not prioritizing my well-being."
- **Why?** "Because I've put myself last for too long, and I want to take control of my health."

Why It Works

By peeling back the layers of your reasoning, you uncover the real driving force behind your dream.

The Reality Check Grid

This technique helps you assess whether your dream is truly realistic by evaluating four key factors: time, resources, skills, and mindset.

Instructions

1. Divide a sheet of paper into four quadrants and label them:
    - **Time:** "How much time can I realistically dedicate to this goal?"

- **Resources:** "What tools, finances, or external support do I need?"
      - **Skills:** "Do I have the necessary skills? If not, what do I need to learn?"
      - **Mindset:** "What mental blocks or fears might hold me back?"
  2. Fill in each quadrant honestly. If there are gaps, brainstorm ways to address them.

Example for learning a new skill:

- **Time:** "I can commit 30 minutes a day, five days a week."
- **Resources:** "I have access to free online courses."
- **Skills:** "I need to improve my time management to stay consistent."
- **Mindset:** "I'm afraid of failing, so I need to practice self-compassion."

Why It Works

This method keeps your dreams grounded in reality. Instead of setting yourself up for failure, you create an actionable plan that acknowledges potential obstacles and provides solutions.

The "5 Second Rule" Exercise

Inspired by Mel Robbins's 5 Second Rule, this technique combats hesitation and self-doubt by pushing you into action before your brain has time to talk you out of it (Robbins, 2017).

Instructions

1. When you feel resistance toward taking action, count down: 5-4-3-2-1—GO!
2. Immediately take a small step toward your dream, whether that's sending an email, making a decision, or starting a task.
3. Use this technique whenever procrastination, fear, or overthinking tries to take over.

Why It Works

This rule interrupts negative thought patterns and prevents hesitation from turning into avoidance (Robbins, 2017). It rewires your brain to take action before doubt sets in.

The "Success Journaling" Exercise

Often, people focus on what they haven't accomplished, which reinforces feelings of failure. Success Journaling shifts your focus to what has gone right, rewiring your brain to recognize progress.

Instructions

1. Every evening, write down three things you did well that day, no matter how small.
2. Reflect on any progress you made toward your dream, even if it was just taking one step.
3. Note what you learned and how you can improve the next day.

Why It Works

By documenting successes, you create positive reinforcement that counteracts self-doubt. Over time, this practice shifts your mindset from "I'm not doing enough" to "I am making progress."

The "Fear Setting" Exercise

Fear is one of the biggest barriers. This practice, popularized by Tim Ferriss, helps you confront fears by breaking them down logically (Lawrence, 2023).

Instructions

1. Write down your goal and identify the worst-case scenario if you fail.
2. Ask yourself: How likely is this outcome, and how could I recover if it happened?

3. Write down all the potential benefits of taking action despite fear.
4. Consider the cost of *not* pursuing your goal—what will you lose if you let fear hold you back?

Why It Works

Fear-setting exposes irrational worries and replaces them with a rational action plan. It also highlights that inaction often has greater consequences than taking a risk.

The "10-10-10 Method" Exercise

This exercise, developed by Suzy Welch, helps you make better decisions about your goals by assessing their long-term impact. Often, self-doubt arises when you fear making the wrong choice. The 10-10-10 Method provides a structured way to evaluate the consequences of your actions (Chang, 2025).

Instructions

1. Identify a purpose or decision you are struggling with (e.g., "Should I commit to a daily workout?").
2. Ask yourself three questions:
    - *How will I feel about this decision in 10 minutes?*
    - *How will I feel about it in 10 months?*
    - *How will I feel about it in 10 years?*
3. Write down your answers and analyze them. If the long-term benefits outweigh the short-term discomfort, you know it's a dream worth pursuing.

Why It Works

This method shifts your perspective from immediate emotions to long-term impact. It helps you push through temporary discomfort, knowing that your future self will thank you for staying committed (Chang, 2025).

The "Two-Minute Rule" Exercise

Procrastination often prevents people from taking action. The Two-Minute Rule eliminates this barrier by making it ridiculously easy to start.

Instructions

1. Choose a plan that feels overwhelming (e.g., "Write a book").
2. Break it down into the smallest possible action that takes two minutes or less (e.g., "Write one sentence" or "Open my document").
3. Commit to doing just that small action. If you feel like continuing, great. If not, you've still made progress.

Why It Works

Once you start, momentum takes over. Getting started is often the hardest part, but this method removes that resistance.

The "Failure Reframing" Exercise

Failure often triggers self-doubt and discouragement, but what if you viewed it as a learning tool instead of a setback? This technique helps you shift your mindset by analyzing failures in a constructive way.

Instructions

1. Think of a past failure related to goal-setting.
2. Write down what went wrong and how it made you feel.
3. Now, reframe it—what did you learn from that experience? How can you apply those lessons to your current objective?
4. Create an action plan to use this knowledge in your future efforts.

Why It Works

This method eliminates the fear of failure by turning it into a valuable learning experience. Instead of seeing failure as an endpoint, you begin to view it as a stepping stone toward growth.

The "80/20 Rule" Exercise

The Pareto Principle states that 80% of results come from 20% of efforts. This practice helps you focus on the most impactful actions rather than wasting energy on tasks that don't contribute much to your dream (Tardi, 2023).

Instructions:

1. List all the tasks related to your dream.
2. Identify the 20% of actions that will bring 80% of the results.
3. Prioritize those tasks and spend most of your time on them.
4. Eliminate or delegate low-impact activities that don't contribute significantly to your success.

Why It Works

Many people struggle with progress because they spread themselves too thin. By identifying the key actions that yield the biggest results, you work smarter instead of harder.

Setting and achieving realistic goals provides a sense of accomplishment and direction, keeping negativity at bay. However, progress is not always linear, and setbacks are inevitable. The key is not just making progress but maintaining it. How do you prevent old negative thinking patterns from resurfacing? How do you stay committed to the changes you've made? The final chapter explores strategies for sustaining positive changes, recognizing early warning signs of relapse, and staying on track for the long term.

10

MAINTAINING PROGRESS AND PREVENTING RELAPSE

You've put in the work, challenged your old thought patterns, and built a stronger, more emotionally intelligent mindset. But we all know that growth isn't a straight line. Some days, you'll feel like you've mastered your emotions; on others, you may slip back into overthinking, self-doubt, or negative habits. That's normal. The real question isn't whether setbacks will happen but how you'll respond when they do.

Think of your emotional progress as strengthening a muscle. If you stop exercising, those muscles weaken over time. Similarly, if you stop practicing self-awareness, emotional regulation, and positive thinking, old patterns can creep back in. But just as you can regain physical strength through consistent effort, you can reinforce your emotional resilience with the right strategies.

What triggers your setbacks?

Is it stress, criticism, unexpected failure, or comparison? Maybe it's a subtle shift—skipping your journaling practice, neglecting boundaries, or surrounding yourself with negativity. Identifying these patterns before they take hold is key to staying on track.

In this chapter, we'll explore practical ways to safeguard your progress and build mental safeguards against relapse. You'll learn how to reinforce healthy habits, recognize early warning signs, and develop a mindset that keeps you moving forward even when life tests you.

IMPORTANCE OF ONGOING PRACTICE AND SELF-AWARENESS

Consistency is the backbone of lasting emotional growth. Without ongoing practice and self-awareness, even the strongest progress can fade into old patterns. The mind, much like a well-tended garden, succeeds when nurtured regularly. If left unchecked, weeds of self-doubt, negative thinking, and emotional reactivity can creep back in, undoing the hard work you've put in.

You might have already noticed that emotional intelligence isn't something you achieve once and never think about again; it requires active engagement. The way you think, react, and interpret the world is shaped by years of conditioning. Overcoming those deeply ingrained patterns isn't a one-time event; it's a process that requires regular maintenance. Without it, the progress you've made can gradually erode, leading to setbacks that feel frustrating and discouraging.

But, slipping up doesn't mean starting over from scratch. It simply means recalibrating, paying attention to what triggered the setback, and using your emotional tools to regain control.

The Power of Small, Daily Reinforcements

Sustainable change doesn't come from grand gestures but from small, consistent actions. Just like a single workout won't build muscle, one moment of self-awareness won't eliminate negative thought patterns. Instead, it's the daily reinforcements, mindful breathing, positive self-talk, and intentional reflection that create resilience over time.

For example, a simple habit like journaling your thoughts can keep you in tune with your emotional state, helping you catch patterns of overthinking before they get out of control. Likewise, practicing gratitude, even on difficult days, shifts your focus from what's going wrong to what's still within your control. These micro-adjustments act as safeguards, keeping you anchored when life tries to pull you back into negativity.

Another powerful tool is self-questioning. When doubt or fear creeps in, challenge it with a direct question:

- *Is this thought based on fact or assumption?*
- *Am I falling into an old pattern?*
- *Is this a legitimate concern?*

By interrogating your thoughts, you weaken their grip and regain clarity before they derail your progress.

Identifying and Managing Emotional Triggers

Even with strong emotional habits, certain triggers can test your resilience. These may come from external sources (criticism, rejection, uncertainty) or internal ones (perfectionism and comparison). Recognizing what sets you off allows you to respond rather than react.

Let's say someone makes an offhand comment that feels like a personal attack. In the past, you might have given in to overanalyzing their words, replaying the moment endlessly. Now, you have a choice: step back, acknowledge the emotional reaction without letting it consume you, and shift your focus to what truly matters. Instead of thinking, *They must not respect me,* you can reframe it as *Their words don't define me. My worth isn't up for debate.*

Similarly, if stress is a common trigger, pay attention to the early physical and mental signs. Catching these moments early allows you to implement grounding techniques before stress takes control. Be it deep breathing, movement, or stepping away for a mental reset, having a go-to strategy ensures you don't fall into old coping mechanisms like self-criticism or emotional shutdown.

The Danger of Complacency

One of the biggest threats to long-term progress is the illusion of stability. Once you start feeling better, it's easy to assume you no longer need to put in the same effort. But growth isn't about reaching a finish line; it's about continuous refinement.

Imagine a skilled musician who, after mastering an instrument, stops practicing altogether. Over time, their precision dulls, and their ability weakens. Emotional intelligence works the same way. If you stop engaging with your habits, such as self-reflection, boundary-setting, and emotional regulation, your ability to manage challenges diminishes.

Complacency often creeps in subtly. You can skip a mindfulness practice here, let a self-doubting thought slide there, and before you know it, negative patterns start to regain their hold. The best way to combat this is to stay engaged. Keep learning, keep refining, and keep challenging yourself.

Building a Relapse-Resistant Mindset

Preventing relapse does not mean you are going to achieve perfection. It's simply about building a mindset that can withstand setbacks without losing momentum. This means focusing on self-compassion, adjusting expectations, and viewing challenges as opportunities rather than failures.

Self-compassion is especially crucial. Too often, when people experience setbacks, they judge themselves harshly: *I should be better at this by now.* But growth and progress aren't erased by a single misstep. Instead of berating yourself, remind yourself: *This is part of the process. What can I learn from this moment?*

Another powerful strategy is preparing for obstacles in advance. Anticipate situations that might challenge you, such as stressful work deadlines, social pressure, and unexpected failures, and create a plan for handling them. When you already know how you'll respond, you take away their power to throw you off course.

Finally, surround yourself with reinforcement. Whether it's a support system, a set of daily affirmations, or a personal mission statement that reminds you why you started this journey, having external reminders keeps you anchored.

Your progress is worth protecting. And the more intentional you are about maintaining it, the more resilient you become.

STRATEGIES TO SUSTAIN POSITIVE CHANGES AND HANDLE SETBACKS

Sustaining positive change needs more than just awareness; it needs action. You already know that setbacks are part of the journey, but how you respond determines whether they become temporary detours or complete derailments. The right strategies help you stay on track, reinforcing your progress while equipping you to navigate challenges with confidence.

Daily Mental Check-Ins

Your thoughts shape your emotions, and your emotions drive your actions. Without regular self-check-ins, negative thought patterns can sneak back in unnoticed. A daily mental check-in helps you stay aware of your emotional state, ensuring that small stressors don't escalate into full-blown setbacks.

Instructions

1. Set aside 5–10 minutes each day (morning, midday, or evening) to assess your feelings.
2. Ask yourself:
    - *What am I feeling right now?*
    - *What thoughts are dominating my mind?*
    - *Are these thoughts helping or hurting me?*
3. If you notice negative patterns, challenge them with a counter-question:
    - *Is this based on fact or assumption?*

4. End with a positive reinforcement statement, such as: "I am in control of my emotions and my response to challenges."

Why It Works

This practice keeps you emotionally grounded, helping you spot patterns before they become uncontrollable. By addressing negative thoughts in real time, you prevent them from festering and influencing your behavior.

Micro-Habits for Emotional Resilience

Big lifestyle changes can feel overwhelming, making them harder to sustain. Instead, micro-habits (small, easily repeatable actions) help reinforce emotional strength without feeling like a burden.

Instructions

1. Choose one small action that aligns with your emotional goals (writing down one positive thought each morning, practicing gratitude for 30 seconds, or setting a daily intention).
2. Keep it simple and achievable, something that takes no more than a few minutes.
3. Pair it with an existing habit (after brushing your teeth, you write a quick gratitude note).
4. Be consistent, but don't stress about perfection-progress matters more than rigid routines.

Why It Works

Micro-habits create long-term change by making positive behaviors automatic. They require minimal effort but produce lasting benefits, strengthening your emotional foundation over time.

The "Three Wins" Reflection

Setbacks often make you focus on what's going wrong, which can erode confidence. Shifting focus to small wins keeps you motivated and reminds you of your progress.

Instructions

1. At the end of each day, reflect on three things you did well, no matter how small.
2. For example:
    - *I handled a tough conversation calmly.*
    - *I didn't spiral into self-doubt today.*
    - *I made time for self-care.*
3. Write them down or say them out loud before bed.
4. If you struggle to find wins, reframe your perspective:
    - *Did I show up for myself today?*
    - *Did I challenge a negative thought?*

Why It Works

Acknowledging progress, even in small ways, builds momentum. It counteracts self-doubt and strengthens confidence in your ability to handle challenges.

The Reset Ritual for Setbacks

A setback means a signal to recalibrate. Having a structured reset ritual helps you bounce back without getting stuck in guilt or frustration.

Instructions

1. When you recognize a setback, pause instead of reacting emotionally.
2. Take three deep breaths to reset your nervous system.
3. Ask yourself:
    - *What triggered this?*
    - *What can I learn from it?*
4. Reaffirm your commitment to progress:
    - *This moment doesn't define me. I know how to move forward.*
5. Take one small positive action immediately, whether it's journaling, taking a walk, or reaffirming a personal mantra.

Why It Works

This approach removes the emotional weight of setbacks and shifts your focus to action rather than self-blame. It trains your brain to see challenges as learning experiences, making future setbacks easier to handle.

The "Who Am I Becoming?" Perspective Shift

Rather than focusing only on short-term challenges, shift your mindset to the bigger picture, who you are becoming through this process.

Instructions

1. When faced with self-doubt, ask:
   - *If I were already the best version of myself, how would I handle this?*
2. Visualize your future self as confident, emotionally strong, and resilient.
3. Make decisions based on the person you're becoming, not the person you've been.
4. Use this perspective when making choices about habits, reactions, and mindset shifts.

Why It Works

This strategy helps you step out of short-term frustration and align with your long-term growth. It shifts your focus from immediate struggles to the bigger vision of self-improvement.

"Emotional Budgeting"—Allocating Your Mental Energy Wisely

Just like financial budgeting prevents overspending, emotional budgeting ensures that you don't exhaust your mental energy on things that don't serve you.

Instructions

1. Every morning, visualize your emotional energy as a limited budget for the day. For example, imagine that you have 100 emotional currency points.
2. Assign point values to different activities. For instance, if you are arguing online, 30 points. Similarly, if you are worrying about something you can't change, 40 points. Are you spending time in nature? 10 points.)
3. Be mindful of where you're "spending" your energy and adjust if you're investing too much in draining activities.

Why It Works

This technique creates awareness around emotional exhaustion and helps you prioritize energy for things that contribute to growth rather than depletion.

"Decision-Free Mornings" for Mental Clarity

Decision fatigue and making too many small decisions early in the day can drain mental energy and make emotional regulation harder. Simplifying morning choices conserves energy for more important tasks.

Instructions

1. Reduce unnecessary morning decisions by setting routines: pre-planned outfits, meals, and even a structured morning schedule.
2. Stick to a consistent morning ritual (for example, wake up, stretch, hydrate, and start your day without excessive decision-making).
3. Reserve decision-making energy for emotionally important challenges later in the day.

Why It Works

Reducing small decisions early in the day keeps your mental bandwidth available for challenges that actually require emotional resilience, making setbacks easier to handle.

The "Bad Day Insurance" Strategy

No matter how much progress you make, some days will be tougher than others. The "Bad Day Insurance" strategy involves preparing for difficult days in advance so that when they come, you don't give in to negativity.

Instructions

1. Write yourself a letter or record a voice note on a good day, reminding yourself of your strengths, past victories, and why setbacks don't define you.
2. Store this in an accessible place (a journal, phone notes, or a voice memo).
3. On tough days, revisit this message to remind yourself of your resilience and perspective.

Why It Works

Sentiments cloud rational thinking in difficult moments. Having a pre-written message from your past self provides a grounding force, helping you stay connected to your long-term progress rather than reacting emotionally to temporary challenges.

"The Rule of Thirds" for Managing Setbacks

The Rule of Thirds is a concept borrowed from elite athletes, who understand that not every day will feel successful, and that's okay (Smith, 2024).

Instructions

1. Accept that, in any given week, one-third of your days will feel great, one-third will feel neutral, and one-third will feel difficult.
2. Instead of expecting perfection, embrace difficult days as part of the process.
3. When you hit a setback, remind yourself: *This is just part of my "difficult third." Tomorrow could be a better day.*

Why It Works

This removes the pressure of needing to feel "on" every day. When setbacks feel normal rather than failures, they lose their power over you, making it easier to move forward.

The "Three Word Identity" Shift

Most setbacks shake your identity. Instead of letting external challenges define you, create an identity that reinforces resilience and growth. The Three Word Identity technique helps you embody the person you want to be.

Instructions

1. Choose three words that define the strongest, most capable version of yourself. Examples: Resilient, Focused, Confident or Creative, Brave, Compassionate.
2. When facing a setback, act according to these words rather than your emotions.
3. Ask yourself: How would a "Resilient, Focused, Confident" person respond to this moment?
4. Repeat these words daily to reinforce the mindset shift.

Why It Works

Your brain seeks consistency between your identity and actions. When you repeatedly affirm a strong identity, you naturally align your behavior with it.

The Identity-Based To-Do List

Traditional to-do lists focus on tasks, but an identity-based to-do list focuses on behaviors that reinforce your desired self-image.

Instructions

1. Instead of listing tasks, write actions that align with the type of person you want to be.
2. For instance, instead of writing "Meditate today," write "I am someone who prioritizes mindfulness."
3. Each time you check off an item, you're reinforcing that identity.

Why It Works

Shifting from task-based thinking to identity-based thinking strengthens long-term change by making new behaviors feel like a natural part of who you are.

The "Permission to Suck" Mindset

Fear of imperfection often paralyzes progress. The Permission to Suck mindset removes the pressure of needing to be perfect, allowing you to keep moving forward even when things aren't going well.

Instructions

1. When struggling with a setback or feeling stuck, tell yourself:
    - "I give myself permission to do this badly."
2. Instead of focusing on perfection, focus on consistency and action.
3. If you're avoiding a task because of fear (writing, exercising,

speaking up), do a low-pressure version just to keep momentum going.

Why It Works

This technique disarms perfectionism and self-judgment, making it easier to push through difficult moments without quitting.

Maintaining progress is not about perfection; it's about resilience. There will be moments when negativity creeps back in, but with the right strategies, you can catch it early and redirect your thoughts before they get out of control. The journey to overcoming negative thinking is ongoing, but every step you've taken so far has brought you closer to a mindset of clarity, strength, and inner peace. As we reach the conclusion of this book, take a moment to reflect on how far you've come and what it means to fully embrace a life free from the grip of negativity.

CONCLUSION

Overcoming negative thinking is not about achieving a state of constant positivity or eliminating all difficulties in your life. It is about reclaiming control over your mind, knowing that your thoughts are not fixed truths, and learning how to direct them in a way that serves you rather than limits you. It is about breaking free from the cycle of self-doubt, worry, and fear that has kept you stuck and replacing it with a mindset that empowers you to take action, embrace challenges, and build emotional resilience.

By now, you have explored the 10-step blueprint designed to help you identify, challenge, and rewire the thought patterns that have been holding you back. You have learned how negative thinking operates, how it infiltrates your daily life, and how it influences your emotions, decisions, and relationships. More importantly, you have discovered that these thought patterns are not permanent. They are simply habits that have been reinforced over time, but like any habit, they can be changed with conscious effort and persistence.

If there is one truth to take away from this, it is that you are not your thoughts. Thoughts come and go, shaped by past experiences, societal conditioning, and ingrained beliefs, but they do not define you. The power lies in your ability to step back, observe them without judgment, and choose which ones to accept and which ones to release. The more you practice this awareness, the more control you gain over your mental state, and the easier it becomes to redirect your thinking toward something constructive rather than destructive.

The process of rewiring your brain is not immediate. There will be days when old thought patterns resurface, moments when doubt creeps in, and times when it feels like progress is slipping away. This does not mean you have failed. It means you are human. Changing long-standing mental habits requires patience, self-compassion, and the willingness to keep going, even when it feels difficult. Setbacks are not proof that you are incapable of change; they are opportunities to apply what you have learned, to practice resilience, and to reaffirm your commitment to a healthier way of thinking.

Emotional resilience is not the absence of negativity but the ability to navigate it without being consumed by it. Resilience allows you to acknowledge your struggles without letting them define you. It enables you to process difficult emotions without suppressing them, to reframe setbacks as learning experiences rather than failures, and to move forward even in uncertainty. It is not about eliminating fear, doubt, or discomfort but about developing the inner strength to face them without allowing them to dictate your actions.

As you continue on this path, remember that small, consistent efforts lead to lasting change. It is not making one grand change overnight but about the daily choices you make- choosing to challenge a negative thought instead of accepting it as truth, choosing to speak to yourself with kindness rather than criticism, choosing to take action despite fear rather than remaining paralyzed by it. These small decisions accumulate over time, gradually shifting your mindset and reinforcing a new, healthier way of thinking.

Surrounding yourself with the right influences is equally important. Just as negativity is contagious, so is positivity. The people you interact with, the content you consume, and the environments you immerse yourself in all play a role in shaping your thought patterns. Be intentional about the energy you allow into your life. Seek out relationships that uplift and encourage you, engage with material that expands your perspective, and create habits that reinforce the mindset you are cultivating.

There will always be external factors beyond your control, such as unexpected challenges, disappointments, and difficult circumstances. But what you can control is how you respond to them. Your thoughts, your mindset, and your perspective are within your power. When negativity arises, remind yourself that you have the tools to handle it. You are not powerless in the face of your thoughts; you have the ability to shift them, to challenge them, and to replace them with something better.

Inner peace does not guarantee a life free of obstacles but developing the mental clarity and emotional strength to deal with whatever comes your way. It is about freeing yourself from the mental noise that once held you back and developing a sense of balance and confidence that allows you to move through life with greater ease. It is knowing that no matter what challenges arise, you have the resilience, awareness, and mindset to face them.

You have already taken a significant step by committing to this process. The knowledge, strategies, and insights you have gained throughout this book are now part of your mental toolkit. However, knowledge alone is not enough; true and permanent change comes from application. Keep practicing, keep challenging your old thought patterns, and keep reinforcing the beliefs that serve you. The more you integrate these principles into your daily life, the more natural they will become, until eventually, positive thinking and emotional resilience are no longer things you have to force but simply the way you operate.

You are not bound by the limitations of your past thinking. You have the ability to reshape your mind, to rewrite your inner dialogue, and to create a life no longer dictated by negativity and fear. The power to change has always been within you.

Now, it is yours to use.

BIBLIOGRAPHY

- Ackerman, C. (2018, February 12). *Cognitive restructuring techniques for reframing thoughts.* Positive Psychology. https://positivepsychology.com/cbt-cognitive-restructuring-cognitive-distortions/
- *Aquatic therapy:* The healing power of fish watching. (2024, July 22). *Intan Growel.* https://intanaquariumfeeds.com/blogs/articles/aquatic-therapy-the-healing-power-of-fish-watching
- Arlinghaus, K. R., & Johnston, C. A. (2018). The importance of creating habits and routine. *American Journal of Lifestyle Medicine, 13*(2), 142–144. https://www.ncbi.nlm.nih.gov/pmc/articles/PMC6378489/
- Balban, M. Y., Neri, E., Kogon, M. M., Weed, L., Nouriani, B., Jo, B., Holl, G., Zeitzer, J. M., Spiegel, D., & Huberman, A. D. (2023). Brief structured respiration practices enhance mood and reduce physiological arousal. *Cell Reports Medicine, 4*(1). https://doi.org/10.1016/j.xcrm.2022.100895
- Barron, T. (2020, April 20). *The indian breath: 8 types of pranayama breathing techniques and their benefits.* Stresscoach. https://www.stresscoach.app/blog/8-types-of-pranayama-breathing-and-their-benefits/
- Belmont, J. (2017, July 24). *CBT technique: Using the triple column technique to change your thoughts to change your life!* Psych Central. https://psychcentral.com/pro/psychoeducation/2017/07/cbt-technique-using-the-triple-column-technique-to-change-your-thoughts-to-change-your-life#1
- Bentley, T. G. K., Penna, G. D., Rakic, M., Arce, N., LaFaille, M., Berman, R., Cooley, K., & Sprimont, P. (2023). Breathing practices for stress and anxiety reduction: Conceptual framework of implementation guidelines based on a systematic review of the published literature. *Brain Sciences, 13*(12), 1612. https://doi.org/10.3390/brainsci13121612
- *Brené Brown on shame and accountability.* (2020, July 1). Brené Brown. https://brenebrown.com/podcast/brene-on-shame-and-accountability/
- Breznoscakova, D., Sedlakova, E., Pallayova, M., & Kovanicova, M. (2023). Autogenic training in mental disorders: What can we expect? *International Journal of Environmental Research and Public Health, 20*(5), 4344–4344. https://doi.org/10.3390/ijerph20054344
- Camacho, B. (2024, January 25). *Grounding techniques: 17 strategies for coping with anxiety.* Talkiatry. https://www.talkiatry.com/blog/grounding-techniques-anxiety-coping-strategies
- Cassata, C. (2022, May 17). *Michael Phelps: "My depression and anxiety is never going to just disappear."* Healthline. https://www.healthline.com/health-news/michael-phelps-my-depression-and-anxiety-is-never-going-to-just-disappear

- Chang, K. (2025, January 9). *The 10-10-10 rule helps you become your future self now*. The Everygirl. https://theeverygirl.com/10-10-10-rule-for-manifestation/
- Chowdhury, M. R. (2019, April 9). *The neuroscience of gratitude and effects on the brain*. Positive Psychology. https://positivepsychology.com/neuroscience-of-gratitude/
- Conway, S. (2021, January 17). *Name it to tame it: How labelling emotions helps kids manage them*. Mindful Little Minds Psychology. https://www.mindfullittleminds.com/name-it-to-tame-it/
- DePaulo, B. (2014, December 28). Why don't we confide in the people closest to us? *Psychology Today*. https://www.psychologytoday.com/us/blog/living-single/201412/why-dont-we-confide-in-the-people-closest-to-us
- Gibson, J. (2024, April 2). *Be wary: Your brain doesn't know the difference between reality and imagination*. Medium. https://medium.com/illumination/be-wary-your-brain-doesnt-know-the-difference-between-reality-and-imagination-ef10f8accb7f
- Goldminz, I. (2018, September 25). *Emotional reasoning and other cognitive distortions*. Medium. https://www.google.com/search?sca_esv=cd25324f189e683f&rlz=1CALCPY_enPK1152PK1152&sxsrf=AHTn8zqwVIjqH_5N-M70igsMoqm7Rzkv-g:1741764832927&q=By+demanding+proof
- Haghighi, A. S. (2022, September 16). *Tummo breathing: Benefits and how to do it*. Medical News Today. https://www.medicalnewstoday.com/articles/tummo-breathing
- Harvard Health. (2025, January 16). *Benefits of mindfulness*. HelpGuide.org. https://www.helpguide.org/mental-health/stress/benefits-of-mindfulness
- Hofmann, S. G., & Hay, A. C. (2018). Rethinking avoidance: Toward a balanced approach to avoidance in treating anxiety disorders. *Journal of Anxiety Disorders, 55*(55), 14–21. https://doi.org/10.1016/j.janxdis.2018.03.004
- Imagawa, N., Mizuno, Y., Nakata, I., Komoto, N., Sakebayashi, H., Shigetoh, H., Kodama, T., & Miyazaki, J. (2023). The impact of stretching intensities on neural and autonomic responses: Implications for relaxation. *Sensors, 23*(15), 6890. https://doi.org/10.3390/s23156890
- Jäncke, L. (2008). Music, memory and emotion. *Journal of Biology, 7*(6), 21. https://doi.org/10.1186/jbiol82
- Jayasinghe, D. (2024, January 13). *How gratitude can overcome the negativity bias*. Medium. https://djayasi.medium.com/how-gratitude-can-overcome-the-negativity-bias-23f6ddb15ff1
- Jimenez, M. P. (2021). Associations between nature exposure and health: a review of the evidence. *International Journal of Environmental Research and Public Health, 18*(9). https://doi.org/10.3390/ijerph18094790
- Johnson, L. F. (2023, November 9). *How to reduce stress & overwhelm with labeling*. LinkedIn. https://www.linkedin.com/pulse/how-reduce-stress-overwhelm-labeling-lydia-f-johnson-ms-imd0c

- Keng, S. L., Smoski, M. J., & Robins, C. J. (2011). Effects of mindfulness on psychological health: A review of empirical studies. *Clinical Psychology Review, 31*(6), 1041–1056. https://doi.org/10.1016/j.cpr.2011.04.006
- Kop, W. J., Synowski, S. J., Newell, M. E., Schmidt, L. A., Waldstein, S. R., & Fox, N. A. (2011). Autonomic nervous system reactivity to positive and negative mood induction: The role of acute psychological responses and frontal electrocortical activity. *Biological Psychology, 86*(3), 230–238. https://doi.org/10.1016/j.biopsycho.2010.12.003
- Kwok, C., Grisham, J. R., & Norberg, M. M. (2018). Object attachment: Humanness increases sentimental and instrumental values. *Journal of Behavioral Addictions, 7*(4), 1132–1142. https://doi.org/10.1556/2006.7.2018.98
- Lawrence, K. E. (2023, March 7). *How I fight my anxiety using Tim Ferriss' fear-setting technique*. Medium. https://medium.com/masterpieces-in-progress/how-i-fight-my-anxiety-using-tim-ferriss-fear-setting-technique-b575484f44d0
- Luft, C. D. B., Zioga, I., Giannopoulos, A., Di Bona, G., Binetti, N., Civilini, A., Latora, V., & Mareschal, I. (2022). Social synchronization of brain activity increases during eye-contact. *Communications Biology, 5*(1). https://doi.org/10.1038/s42003-022-03352-6
- Madeson, M. (2025, February 22). *Cognitive distortions: 15 examples & worksheets (PDF)*. Positive Psychology. https://positivepsychology.com/cognitive-distortions/
- Martin, E. S. Bromberg-., Matsumoto, M., & Hikosaka, O. (2010). Dopamine in motivational control: Rewarding, aversive, and alerting. *Neuron, 68*(5), 815–834. https://doi.org/10.1016/j.neuron.2010.11.022
- Martin, L., Oepen, R., Bauer, K., Nottensteiner, A., Mergheim, K., Gruber, H., & Koch, S. (2018). Creative arts interventions for stress management and prevention—a systematic review. *Behavioral Sciences, 8*(2), 28. https://doi.org/10.3390/bs8020028
- Marzola, P., Melzer, T., Pavesi, E., Mohapel, J. G. -, & Brocardo, P. S. (2023). Exploring the role of neuroplasticity in development, aging, and neurodegeneration. *Brain Sciences, 13*(12). https://doi.org/10.3390/brainsci13121610
- Mayer, B. A. (2022, January 11). *Candle meditation: Can gazing at a flame increase your focus?* Healthline; Healthline Media. https://www.healthline.com/health/candle-meditation#takeaway
- Naz, S. (2024, November 24). *Rewire your Brain for positive thinking through repetition*. Medium; ILLUMINATION. https://medium.com/illumination/rewire-your-brain-for-positive-thinking-through-repetition-be4912cbd426
- Neff, K. D. (2009). The role of self-compassion in development: A healthier way to relate to oneself. *Human Development, 52*(4), 211–214. https://doi.org/10.1159/000215071
- Niles, A. N., Haltom, K. E. B., Mulvenna, C. M., Lieberman, M. D., & Stanton, A. L. (2013). Effects of expressive writing on psychological and physical

- health: The moderating role of emotional expressivity. *Anxiety, Stress, & Coping, 27*(1), 1–17. https://doi.org/10.1080/10615806.2013.802308
- Oppland, M. (2016, December 16). *8 ways to create flow according to Mihaly Csikszentmihalyi*. PositivePsychology. https://positivepsychology.com/mihaly-csikszentmihalyi-father-of-flow/
- Pearson, J., Naselaris, T., Holmes, E. A., & Kosslyn, S. M. (2015). Mental imagery: Functional mechanisms and clinical applications. *Trends in Cognitive Sciences, 19*(10), 590–602. https://doi.org/10.1016/j.tics.2015.08.003
- Perera, R. (2024, May 14). *The power of movement: Enhancing mental well-being through physical activity*. LinkedIn. https://www.linkedin.com/pulse/power-movement-enhancing-mental-well-being-through-physical-perera-pqike
- Raypole, C. (2024, August 22). *6 pressure points for anxiety relief*. Healthline. https://www.healthline.com/health/pressure-points-for-anxiety
- Ridsdel, J. (2023, June 1). *10 common negative thinking patterns and 5 steps for change*. The Family Centre. https://www.familycentre.org/news/post/10-common-negative-thinking-patterns-and-5-steps-for-change
- Robbins, M. (2017). *The 5 second rule: Transform your life, work, and confidence with everyday courage*. Savio Republic.
- Scott, E. (2020, February 11). *How to practice loving kindness meditation*. Verywell Mind. https://www.verywellmind.com/how-to-practice-loving-kindness-meditation-3144786
- Scott, E. (2024, February 12). *What is body scan meditation?* Verywell Mind. https://www.verywellmind.com/body-scan-meditation-why-and-how-3144782
- Smith, S. (2024, March 4). *Accepting the "rule of thirds" in everyday life and in your fitness training*. Military.com. https://www.google.com/search?q=The+Rule+of+Thirds+is+a+concept+borrowed+from+elite+athletes%2C+who+understand+that+not+every+day+will+feel+successful%2C+and+that%E2%80%99s+okay&rlz=1CALCPY_enPK1152PK1152&sourceid=chrome&ie=UTF-8
- Smoul. (2025, January 29). *Rewire your brain to focus better (Scientifically)*. Medium; Practice in Public. https://medium.com/practice-in-public/how-to-rewire-your-brain-to-focus-better-23336bfce183
- Stanborough, R. J. (2022, October 25). *What are cognitive distortions and how can you change these thinking patterns?* Healthline. https://www.healthline.com/health/cognitive-distortions
- Tardi, C. (2023, December 19). *The 80-20 rule (AKA Pareto principle): What it is, how it works*. Investopedia. https://www.investopedia.com/terms/1/80-20-rule.asp
- Thompson, R. (2020, November 8). *The importance of writing your thoughts down*. Medium. https://www.google.com/search?q=eeing+your+thoughts+written+out+makes+them+easier+to+analyze.&rlz=1CALCPY_enPK1152PK1152&sourceid=chrome&ie=UTF-8
- Tindle, J., & Tadi, P. (2022, October 31). *Neuroanatomy, parasympathetic nervous*

system. PubMed; StatPearls Publishing. https://www.ncbi.nlm.nih.gov/books/NBK553141/
- Toussaint, L., Nguyen, Q. A., Roettger, C., Dixon, K., Offenbächer, M., Kohls, N., Hirsch, J., & Sirois, F. (2021). Effectiveness of progressive muscle relaxation, deep breathing, and guided imagery in promoting psychological and physiological states of relaxation. *Evidence-Based Complementary and Alternative Medicine*, *2021*(1), 1–8. https://doi.org/10.1155/2021/5924040
- Villines, Z. (2023, February 19). *What is the havening technique?* Medical News Today; Medical News Today. https://www.medicalnewstoday.com/articles/havening
- Vinall, M. (2021, March 5). *Can shaking your body help heal stress and trauma? Some experts say yes*. Healthline. https://www.healthline.com/health/mental-health/can-shaking-your-body-heal-stress-and-trauma
- Walsh, C. (2020, February 27). *What the nose knows*. Harvard Gazette. https://news.harvard.edu/gazette/story/2020/02/how-scent-emotion-and-memory-are-intertwined-and-exploited/
- Weaver, D. (2024, October 4). *The myth of multitasking: You can't do two things at once*. LinkedIn. https://www.linkedin.com/pulse/myth-multitasking-you-cant-do-two-things-once-david-weaver-cca-couqe/
- WebMD Editorial Contributors. (2023a, April 29). *What is box breathing?* WebMD. https://www.webmd.com/balance/what-is-box-breathing
- WebMD Editorial Contributors. (2023b, July 27). *What to know about 4-7-8 breathing*. WebMD. https://www.webmd.com/balance/what-to-know-4-7-8-breathing
- Weerapong, P., Hume, P. A., & Kolt, G. S. (2005). The mechanisms of massage and effects on performance, muscle recovery and injury prevention. *Sports Medicine (Auckland, N.Z.)*, *35*(3), 235–256. https://doi.org/10.2165/00007256-200535030-00004
- What is a floating meditation tank? Plus, 9 health benefits. (2024, August 9). Calm Blog. https://www.calm.com/blog/floating-meditation-tank
- Wickramaratne, P. J., Yangchen, T., Lepow, L., Patra, B. G., Glicksburg, B., Talati, A., Adekkanattu, P., Ryu, E., Biernacka, J. M., Charney, A., Mann, J. J., Pathak, J., Olfson, M., & Weissman, M. M. (2022). Social connectedness as a determinant of mental health: A scoping review. *PLoS One*, *17*(10). https://doi.org/10.1371/journal.pone.0275004
- Yim, J. (2016, July 1). *Therapeutic benefits of laughter in mental health: A theoretical review*. The Tohoku Journal of Experimental Medicine. https://pubmed.ncbi.nlm.nih.gov/27439375/

www.ingramcontent.com/pod-product-compliance
Lightning Source LLC
Chambersburg PA
CBHW020936090426
42736CB00010B/1163